If My People Who Are Called Baptists . . .
A Layman's Challenge

Paul Dodd

If My People Who Are Called Baptists . . .

A Layman's Challenge

Paul Dodd

PROVIDENCE HOUSE PUBLISHERS
Franklin, Tennessee

Printed in the United States of America

00   99   98   97   96   5   4   3   2   1

Library of Congress Catalog Card Number: 96-68046

ISBN: 1-881576-85-X

Cover design by Ernie Hickman

Published by
PROVIDENCE HOUSE PUBLISHERS
238 Seaboard Lane • P.O. Box 158
Franklin, Tennessee 37067
800-881-5692

CONTENTS

PREFACE

THE MOST HAUNTING CHALLENGE EVER RECORDED IS found in 2 Chronicles 7:14: "If my people, who are called by my name, will humble themselves and pray and seek my face and turn from their wicked ways, then will I hear from heaven and will forgive their sin and will heal their land" (NIV). This tells us that if we, who have a personal relationship with God and claim the name of Christ, have a contract with our Creator and Sustainer, and if we are living up to our end of the bargain, the world in which we live will be a much better place.

This book is my personal challenge to every Christian, and particularly to every Christian called Baptist, to find God's plan for your life, live within that plan, and, thus, make a difference in the world. I am a Baptist for at least two reasons. First, I was born to devout Baptist parents and raised in the Baptist tradition. Second, I have had many years to consider other communities of faith and compare them to my Baptist convictions. I have great respect for other denominations and groups, but I am now a Baptist by choice.

My choice to remain a Baptist has been made based on three factors. First, I believe strongly in the priesthood of all believers—the right of every individual to have a personal relationship with God through Christ, without human mediation, which is a long-standing Baptist teaching. Second, I believe in the equality of believers, which is reflected in democratic, congregational rule in Baptist congregations and denominations. And third, I believe in the principles which our Baptist foreparents advocated and gave us as a heritage in this country: freedom of religion and separation of church and state.

7

My concern comes, though, when I look around us and see that, although there are so many of us, there are still so many things wrong in the world. Hunger, crime, disease, and war give ample evidence that our land is not healed. Why is our land not healed? Is it our fault or God's fault? I think we know the answer.

Wouldn't it be wonderful to live in the world as it would be if we Christians were doing what God calls us to do in 2 Chronicles? The best way I know to address this issue is to try to get my own attention and that of the people who are most like me, God's people who are called Baptists, and motivate us to take a harsh, critical look at our lives, change what needs to be changed, and let God make the world a better place through us.

Second Chronicles tells us that it is the religious people, not the skeptics or nonbelievers, who must turn from their "wicked ways" if God is going to "heal our land." This is a bitter pill for us to swallow. I do not know of any person who bears the name of Christian, let alone a Baptist, who would plead guilty to being "wicked." That is an awful word. Yet, we need to admit to the wickedness that we harbor among us, and accept God's call to turn from it.

In this book, I deal with only a few of our "wickednesses." All of them are things which I, as a Baptist, have had to face. These include Baptist legalism, racial bigotry, discrimination against women, letting humans get between us and God, clinging to the past and missing the opportunities of the present and future, saddling ourselves with "stumbling-block" adjectives, failing to study God's revelation through the things he has made, and refusing to live in harmony according to God's plan.

I know that you will not agree with all of my conclusions; I hope that you will not. I do not want you to agree with me. What I do want you to do is to think, rethink, discuss, and think again about our wickedness and our need to change. I want you to talk about these issues with your neighbors, your friends, your family members, your Bible study group, and your pastor.

I want us to humble ourselves, pray, and seek the leadership of God in our lives so that we and the millions of others just like us can turn from our wicked ways and be the blessing to the world that God is waiting for us to be. Spiritual progress can then take place.

1 ... Would See Jesus in Others

LET ME TELL YOU ABOUT MY GRANDDAUGHTER, LISA. SHE IS eight years old and has more energy and ambition than anyone I have ever seen. She has always been able to out think, out run, and out maneuver everyone else, especially me.

Year before last, when she was six, her hockey team was playing against a team from Canada, and she was the only girl on the ice. Some of the Canadian team's fans, seeing a ponytail flying out from what they assumed to be a boy's helmet, started yelling, "Hey, kid! Get a haircut!" In just a matter of seconds, she stole the puck from the other team and began streaking on a breakaway toward the other goal as the home crowd chanted, "Lisa, Lisa, Lisa!"

I drove by her school recently and saw a group of second graders playing football. Guess who was the only girl in the formation, and guess who was quarterback?

I have seen a fierce spirit and competitive nature in this little girl from the day she was born. It seems as if she came into this world with the determination to run faster, hit harder, climb higher, learn more, and otherwise out achieve everyone in sight.

I saw Lisa on the television news the other night. I knew it was Lisa as surely as I was sitting there, although the girl on the screen had a different skin color and hair texture than Lisa, and although she was in very strange surroundings halfway around the world. Despite these differences, however, there on the screen was Lisa moving frantically at the front of a group of refugees, trying desperately to escape death from the hands of a pursuing terrorist army.

I saw Lisa in that newscast because I instantly recognized that this was exactly how Lisa would react if she was faced with the same horrible situation. I saw that same fierce look of determination in the little girl's eyes. I saw evidence of a great rush of adrenaline. I saw frenetic energy being expended.

But what made this situation so sickeningly tragic was that, instead of just trying to win a game, this little girl was running for her very life, hopping on her one remaining leg and using a stick as a single crude crutch.

The image of that desperate little girl has haunted me terribly since I viewed it. I see her as I go to sleep. I see her when I am driving alone. I see her now as I write. I simply cannot forget that precious little girl, nor can I separate her from Lisa in my mind.

My Lisa and the "Lisa" on the screen were obviously endowed by God with similar abilities, instincts, ambitions, and hopes. But the "Lisa" on the newscast had been mutilated by war. Her future was either immediate death or an indeterminate lifetime of coping with a serious physical handicap, fighting for food, searching for a safe place to rest, living in abject poverty, and facing untold other problems—all of this at the age of six or seven, and probably without any surviving family members to even hug or reassure her.

Why was it so easy for me to see Lisa in that little girl? Because I love Lisa! Because I know her! Because I spend time with her! Because I want her to succeed! Because whatever makes her happy makes me happy and whatever causes her pain causes me pain! Because we communicate! Because we have a relationship! After all, we are closely related!

Lisa's brother, Jeremy, is our oldest grandchild. Jeremy became our grandson when our son, Doug, married Jeremy's mother, Paula, when Jeremy was two years old.

"Grandma" Rose, my wife, provided day care for Jeremy during the first couple of years of Doug and Paula's marriage while they both worked so they could afford each other. My work schedule often permitted me to get home from work before Doug and Paula arrived, so Jeremy and I got to spend a lot of time together.

I found that Jeremy and I were kindred spirits, both having a great love for the out-of-doors. He became my instant comrade in gardening and landscaping. We did not need faith to move a mountain. All we needed was a wheelbarrow and two shovels. He would work as long and hard on a project as I would. The only thing that would distract him was when we discovered a bug or worm or other critter that needed to be studied. When this happened, we were equally willing to lay down our tools and give our complete attention to yet another wonder of nature.

Rose and I moved into a new house, in a new neighborhood, when Jeremy was about three years old. We quickly became good friends with our next-door neighbors, Don and Mary Ann.

One day after observing Jeremy and me with our wheelbarrow and shovels, first digging, then taking Jeremy for joyrides in the wheelbarrow, then digging some more, Don remarked to Mary Ann that Jeremy sure looked like his grandfather. After Mary Ann told Rose about this the next day, she was surprised when Rose told her that Jeremy and I were not blood relatives. "But they look so much alike," Mary Ann said. "Jeremy even walks like Paul and acts like Paul."

I do not think that I was ever prouder of anything. Our neighbors saw me in Jeremy. I was never so flattered.

Jesus was pretty clear about his expectations for his followers. He wants us to see him in others, all others, and at all times. We know that this is his standard for being a Christian; yet we do not seem to spend much time or effort trying to meet this standard.

My cousin Betty, who lives in Salt Lake City, is a few years older than I. I had not seen her for forty years until I was in Salt Lake City on business and called her so we could meet and have lunch together.

The last time I had seen Betty was soon after her marriage, when she was in her early twenties and I was a teenager. She was a beautiful young woman with an extraordinary face. I remember that the first time I saw a picture of Marilyn Monroe's face, I thought, "She looks a lot like my cousin Betty."

Halfway through lunch, I just stared at her and said, "Betty, I love your face." When she asked me why, my answer had nothing to do with Marilyn Monroe. My answer was, "When I look at your face, I can see your mother, your father, my mother, our Aunt Maude, our Aunt Lura, and both my sisters. Your face is a family portrait." Her face had been transformed over the years from the beautiful face of a movie star into an even more beautiful face that reflected familiar family characteristics which were so precious to me.

My parents and my two brothers are all dead, but I get glimpses of them in my children and grandchildren. My son Mike is so much like my dad that sometimes I have thought that the reason God put me on this earth was to be the transition person between these two similar personalities. Mike doesn't look like Dad as much as he sounds like him, acts like him, and possesses similar strengths, weaknesses, ailments, and values.

Anytime I am with either of my sons, Doug or Mike, I get fleeting glimpses of my brothers in a furrowed brow, a display of humor, a look of determination, or a voracious appetite. As long as we are near to some of our family, we are near to all of our family.

But this is not enough. As Christians, we are part of another family, the family of God. In this family we have a Father and an older Brother. Paul tells us in Romans that if we are children of God, we are joint heirs with Jesus Christ. That puts us squarely in the middle of the most important family in the whole world.

Think about it. The Creator and Cause-force of the universe has chosen to include us in his family. We became members of this family through the initiative of God the Father. He wanted us in his family. His means of communicating this to us was to send his Son to explain it to us and to pay off all our debts so we could come into the family free and clear.

As we choose to accept this great gift and privilege, we begin to become acquainted with our new older Brother and our Heavenly Father. Unfortunately, this is where some of us want the family relationship to stop.

We may even bask in our small family situation. We read the Bible and pray regularly, live pious "separated" lives, and get involved with a few like-minded people in a church. As we "grow spiritually," we may begin to tithe, hold church offices, and even reach the ultimate in Baptist "spiritual maturity"—sharing with others what we believe.

What is wrong with this picture? Jesus, our big Brother, came into a world that sounds a lot like what I have just described. He came into a society that put great emphasis on reading the Bible, praying, living pious lives, attending religious services, tithing, and making a great show of what they believed. Wow! How could Jesus have possibly found fault with that situation? That, after all, is what most of us Baptists are striving for.

Jesus argued with the high and mighty religious leaders. He chased merchants and money changers out of the Temple. He described some prominent priests as hypocrites. He said that some very religious people were swallowing camels but choking on gnats. He said that those people were so nit-picky that they were looking for specks in other people's eyes while they had two-by-fours in their own eyes. Can you believe that he was not even impressed by tithers? What in the world was wrong? What was he looking for?

In Luke 18 we read about a devout young man, whom we call "the rich young ruler," who came to Jesus just to ask him these very questions. The young man and Jesus discussed his religious life and Jesus pointed out one thing that was missing. The man simply had not recognized that poor people were a part of his family. And, when confronted with this fact, he apparently refused to accept it even though Jesus, himself, pointed it out to him.

Jesus seems to want us to be aware of a family somewhat larger than just ourselves, himself, the Heavenly Father, and our little church crowd. At least, according to that episode, our family must include the poor people of the world.

How does this apply to us Baptists? I have a completely unsubstantiated figure running around in my brain that each Baptist contributes an average of about seventy cents a year to combat world hunger. Of course, that is probably not me or you, but despite Jesus' clear message that the poor are in our family and therefore our responsibility, there must be some Baptists out there who are ruining our average.

How can this be? It is obvious that we are not letting the Holy Spirit guide our vision or our thoughts as we look at the poor of this world. If we were, we would see our older Brother, Jesus, in them. He became poor for our sakes, so that we, in turn, would humble ourselves in order to help meet the needs of others.

God chose for his Son to be born in a part of the world that was suffering from repression, suppression, and depression. Rather than come into the world in an upper-class family, God chose a poor family for his Son. Rather than choose a palace, an inn, or even a house as the site for his Son's birth, God chose a stable. Rather than seek power, wealth, or security, Christ chose to take upon himself the role of a suffering servant.

When we see someone living in poverty, we should see our older Brother in that situation, for he experienced what that person is going through. Perhaps more importantly, he also experiences it with the person right now. Christ cares for all people.

Paul described himself as a debtor to others because of what God had done for him. If God has called us, saved us, and equipped us, it is because he wants us to carry out his will in the world.

God's purpose for his people is much more than the narrow practice of religion that Jesus saw during his earthly life, and it is much more than the narrow practice of religion with which we are often content. God's purpose is for us to see Jesus in others and to help those who are in need.

We do not fulfill God's mission for us by our church activities. They are merely the starting point. The church is our filling station, our energizer, but not our mission. Our mission is the world, and the world is mostly outside the church.

Matthew 9 contains a marvelous record of a brief segment of Jesus' earthly ministry. During one of his trips through the countryside, he visited sinners, healed the sick, raised the dead, preached, taught, and cast out demons until he was exhausted. Still, when he saw a multitude of people with unfulfilled needs who wanted his attention, he felt compassion for them.

What did others see? What did the disciples see? What would we have seen? In all likelihood, we, just like those around Jesus, would probably have had some reaction other than compassion. The natural response of a tired, overworked person to a crowd of needy, demanding people is to be impatient, judgmental, and even resentful.

We hear comments like: "They should solve their own problems." "I have enough to do just to take care of myself." "They should get a job." "We need stricter laws to control these people." Or, one of my favorites, "If we try to help them, we will just make things worse!" Such statements show little compassion.

We might look at the crowd and see skin color, ethnicity, denominations, unbelievers, lazy people, cheats, deadbeats, drunks, addicts, thieves, prostitutes, murderers, the incurably ill, and the hopelessly disadvantaged. If that is all we see as we look at the multitudes around us, we can be sure that we are not looking to see our family member, Jesus, in any of them. We can also be sure that our vision is not being directed by the Holy Spirit who can help us see people as our Heavenly Father sees them.

Matthew tells us that Jesus was "moved with compassion" as he looked at the crowd. My scholar friends tell me that the original text says that he suffered in his inner being and felt pain deep in his stomach and bowels. Why? Because of his identification with, and concern for, the needs, pain, and suffering of others.

Can you relate to this? I can, because that is exactly how I felt as I watched the desperate efforts of that little girl on the evening news, so much like Lisa, as she fled for her life using every ounce of strength she had. But, I am sad to admit, I do not experience this pain equally for everyone who is in need.

I know what the term "compassion" means, but I need to let the Holy Spirit guide my vision rather than rely on my own understanding when confronted with those "family members" whom I do not know or whom I have not taken the time to understand. I think that we need to join the rich young ruler in going to Jesus and asking the question, "What are we doing wrong?" If we do, we may first discover that we have a lot in common with the young ruler. We would rather keep what we have than follow the leading of our big Brother and our Heavenly Father.

As a result, we come up with every rationalization under the sun to justify a self-centered life. We are sure that we have accepted all the gifts that God's grace provides, but we fail to join Paul in seeing that this makes us a debtor to other people. We pray, "forgive us our trespasses as we forgive those who trespass against us," seeking to receive God's forgiveness, but neglecting to give our forgiveness to others.

Second, we may see that we sometimes fall into the same trap as the Pharisees; we become so religious that we are of no benefit to anyone else. We often are so self-satisfied with the Baptist rituals of Bible study, prayer, church attendance, tithing, and witnessing that we stop there. We either do not look upon the multitude with compassion or, if there is a hint of compassion, it consists only of a fleeting thought that they all need to be saved. I hope it troubles you as much as it does me to realize just how far we are from Jesus' example and how close we are to the attitude of the Pharisees.

Third, we may find out that we just do not see the image of Jesus in others like we should. Is that because we do not know him well enough? I would never have seen my mother's image in the face of my cousin if I was not well acquainted with what my mother's face looked like. I can recognize my father's mannerisms in Mike only if I clearly remember how Dad walked and talked. Because I have clear memories of my brothers, I can see them in Doug and Mike.

As Baptists, we know a lot about Jesus, but how well do we really know Jesus? What makes him hurt deep inside? How does he view situations facing us, our church, and our society? What would he do if he were here? As his representative on earth, is that what I am doing?

How would Jesus deal with the homeless, AIDS sufferers, the unemployed, the millions of hungry people, the mentally ill, refugees, single mothers, welfare recipients, the disadvantaged old, the hopeless young, and gang members? The list could go on and on.

But one thing is for sure: some Baptist somewhere has looked at each of the mentioned groups and found some reason why God does not want him or her to minister to those people and, thus, has left them alone. If God's people who are called Baptists would see Jesus in others, what difference would it make in the world?

Let's just choose one small, non-controversial, hypothetical case and think about it. Have you ever thought about the difference it would make if we Baptists refused to have anything to do with a commodity, like, say, maybe, oh, tobacco?

Baptists and tobacco have been intertwined throughout most of this country's history. We smoke it, chew it, dip it, grow it, harvest it, dry it, research it, process it, lobby for it, advertise it, buy it, and sell it. Tobacco is the main source of income for thousands of Baptist families and, in turn, hundreds of Baptist churches.

I have been acquainted with tobacco all my life. I consider myself fortunate that I have never become addicted to it, although it has affected my life in some ways. My father smoked from when he was a teenager until his mid-fifties. Mom once told me that she had made a mistake by not insisting that Dad quit smoking before she married him. But, she said, she had made him give up drinking before the wedding. And, besides, she was sure that, as much as he loved her, all she would have to say after the wedding was, "Honey, why don't you stop smoking?" and that would do it.

So for the next thirty-five years, she kept asking, "Honey, why don't you stop smoking?" until he finally did. Dad probably added years to his life by quitting when he did, yet when he died at age eighty-three, the cause of death was a hemorrhage of the lungs.

I never knew a Baptist pastor who was not a heavy tobacco user until I was a teenager. The brief intermission between Sunday School and the worship service at the Griffith Creek Baptist Church was a time for the men of the church to go out under the big oak trees and have a smoke. That practice continues in many churches today.

Joe Smith, the preacher who married me to my beautiful wife, Rose, was famous for his defense of the use of tobacco. "I am going to chew tobacco and preach the gospel," Brother Joe told his Pentecostal preacher critics, "while you birds chew the gospel and preach tobacco." Is it any wonder that this man was my hero?

My father-in-law and my brother-in-law, Elmer, are confirmed tobacco chewers. One day at my in-laws' home, as Elmer and "Grandpa" were sitting, chewing, and spitting into their soup cans, my mother-in-law and sister-in-law were expressing some disgust at the scene. I wondered aloud to the two women if there would be chewing tobacco in heaven. "I sure hope they have a little bit, don't you, Grandpa?" was Elmer's unsolicited response.

During the last few years, I have become pretty well acquainted with one of the most dreaded words in the English language: Cancer! My wife, Rose, nearly lost her life in an automobile accident that turned out to be, in the words of her doctor, "serendipitous." Although I had lived through the sixties, I still had to look up the word "serendipitous" to find that it means "a gift from God." Rose's accident was serendipitous because, while the surgeons were operating on her to save her life, they discovered that she was in the early stages of lymphoma. With lymphoma, as with any cancer, early detection is crucial. Thank God, her chemotherapy treatments, bolstered by the prayers of many—or was it the other way around?—resulted in the remission of the lymphoma.

One of Rose's most faithful supporters during her crisis was her "baby" sister Judy. Although two hundred fifty miles separated us, Judy was there for us. She came often and stayed as long as she was needed. Then, one fateful day, we got a call from Judy that she, too, had been diagnosed with lymphoma. We soon discovered that, despite massive doses of chemotherapy and ceaseless prayer, she was not going into remission.

During Rose's personal crisis, she had often speculated as to why God had let her survive the horrible accident only to learn that she had cancer. She soon began speculating that perhaps it was God's purpose to equip her so she could be of some help to others who were facing similar problems. Little did she know that, even before her own chemotherapy treatments were completed, she would be needed to minister to her terminally ill baby sister.

Rose was faithful to Judy and to what she now clearly recognized as God's call, despite her own weakened condition. She spent hours on the telephone with Judy and, when possible, we went to Springfield, Massachusetts, to be with Judy and her family.

During one of our visits, while Rose was with Judy in her room in the cancer wing of the hospital, Judy's husband, Gerald, and I stood in the hall and just vented our hatred of cancer to each other. This horrible disease, by threatening the lives of the two persons that we each loved most, was also nearly destroying our lives. We could see the devastating impacts of the illness of two mothers on their children.

We wondered what possible causes could have resulted in two sisters having the same kind of cancer at the same time. Could it be genetic, or something eaten, or a pollutant in the air or water, or a cosmetic that had been used? If we could only determine the cause, surely that cause could be eliminated.

As we were venting, two beautiful girls of college age went past us into the room that their mother shared with Judy. "That is a sad situation there," Gerald commented. "The mother of those girls is forty-nine years old and has advanced lung cancer. She is going to be released tomorrow, and they are going to take her home to die. Do you know what that woman told me would be the best thing about getting home? She would be able to have a cigarette. And she knows that is what got her into this situation in the first place."

We continued to stand there in the hall of the cancer ward and listen to the sounds. A continuous cacophony of coughing, choking, gurgling, and labored breathing sounded throughout the ward.

I commented to Gerald that "every smoker in the country should have to stand here where we are. If they did, surely they would take steps to stop killing themselves."

But then I wondered what God's people could do to improve this situation of horrible suffering and death. And now I am wondering with you as to what we Baptists can do.

First, let's get back to the theme of this chapter: seeing Jesus in others. Do we see Jesus in the suffering, terminally ill, forty-nine-year-old mother who can't wait to get home to have a cigarette? If we do, then what do we do about it? Surely we pray for her, seek to make her last days as comfortable as possible, and, as best we can, share her suffering with her and her family. Even if the sufferer was Jesus, himself, instead of one of his sisters, we could do little more.

Do we see Jesus in the impressionable teenager who is faced with the temptation to start using tobacco? We do if we see Jesus in our own children and grandchildren. If we do, then what do we do about it?

If we truly see Jesus in his teenage brother or sister, we may not want to develop advertising materials which will encourage him or her to start on a path which could lead to an early death and untold suffering. Do we look at the teenager and see Jesus, or a potential customer?

What if every one of us Baptists who has any part in the gigantic tobacco industry would go directly to the Lord, just like the rich young ruler did, and ask him to validate our religious life? What if, after we tell him of our church activities, our missionary efforts, our evangelism, etc., he says, "One thing is lacking, divest yourselves of any interest in, or contact with, tobacco."

Would our answer be different from the one given by the rich young ruler? The Bible said that he departed sadly because he had great possessions. Oh yes, one other thing, there was no evidence cited that his possessions were injuring anyone.

We all know what the rich young ruler should have done. What would have happened to him if he had followed the advice of the Master? He would have used his resources to ease the suffering of many of the poor of his society. He would have had to rely more on God instead of himself, and he would have lived his life by faith rather than by sight. And, most importantly, he would have gone beyond being a religious person and would have become a "follower" of Christ.

Similarly, we all know, deep down, what God's people who are called Baptists should do. There is no way that anyone of us can justify any aspect of an activity that we know causes harm to any of "the least of these." So why do we continue to wrap ourselves in religiosity and rationalize our sin? We do it for the exact same reason that the rich young ruler rejected Jesus' advice. We have "great possessions." The reason is purely economic.

What would happen if we did get totally out of the tobacco industry, as producers, providers, or users, as some Baptists have already done? Our own children would live longer. This one is easy. Just look at the life expectancy of other religious groups that do not use tobacco.

We would be freed from the burden that we are now carrying, knowing that what we are doing is causing pain and suffering in other people. And now that you have read this far, you realize more clearly that when we do it to them, we are doing it to Christ.

We would experience economic loss. We would be in the same boat as the rich young ruler if he had decided to divest himself of his riches. We would have to trust God more and our acreage allotment, or our position, or our retirement system, less.

We would have to live more by faith and less by sight. We would experience spiritual gain and receive the spiritual satisfaction that comes from doing what we know God wants us to do. Remember, the great Teacher said that "man does not live by bread alone."

We would set an example for the world to see. They would know we are Christians because we have love for others. Maybe others would follow our example.

Tobacco is just one of many, many topics that could be similarly discussed. Tobacco is not the issue. Seeing Jesus in others is the issue. Every day of our lives, we face the same dilemma that the rich young ruler faced. What do we see when we look upon the poor, the disadvantaged, the sick, the disenfranchised? Do we, like the Pharisee, thank God that we are not like others or do we, as true followers of the Master, see Jesus in others?

2 . . . WOULD GET READY FOR THE JUDGMENT

MY MATERNAL GRANDFATHER, GEORGE WASHINGTON MEADOR, was a circuit-riding Methodist preacher during the late 1800s and early 1900s in the mountains of southern West Virginia. A lot of stories have been told about the experiences of old-time Methodist and Baptist preachers like him in rural America. Although most of the stories centered around Sunday dinner and the last piece of chicken, one dealt with another subject that I particularly liked.

As the story goes, my grandfather had been named pastor for a new charge or group of small churches. Prior to preaching in a rural church for the first time, Brother George, as he was called, made a practice of riding through the community on his horse to acquaint himself with some of the folks and do a little evangelism. As he rode along, he came upon a man near a farmhouse and stopped to talk.

> "Good morning, sir, I am Brother George Meador and I am the new pastor for the church here. May I ask you, sir, are you a Christian?" Grandpa had a reputation for getting right to the subject.

> "No," the man replied, "my name's Smith. A family by the name of Christian lives on a farm out the ridge about a mile. They must be the ones you are looking for."

> "No, no!" my grandfather said. "You misunderstand me. Are you ready for the judgment?"

"Can't rightly say, preacher," Mr. Smith responded. "When is it gonna be?"

This made Grandpa spit and sputter. "Who knows?" he said. "It might be today, it might be tomorrow, or it might be next week. It could be anytime!"

"Well, when you get the time set, you let us know," Mr. Smith said. "I have an idea that my wife will want to pack a lunch and spend the day."

I clearly remember hearing, as a child, a powerful sermon preached by an evangelist during a revival meeting about the Great White Throne Judgment. His description of that terrible event had me on the edge of my seat until he told us that if we were saved, we did not have to worry about it.

The terrifying Great White Throne Judgment spoken of in Revelation, he told us, is going to be only for the unsaved. Those of us who have accepted Christ will not be there. We will have our day in court at the much more pleasant Judgment Seat of Christ, where all the rewards will be passed out. This was quite a relief!

The only thing that we have to fear is that some bad thing we have done might come up at the Judgment Seat, and God will frown; but then Jesus will say, "I died for that person," and all will be well. The only question we will be asked will be, "Did you accept Christ as your personal Savior?" And, of course, we did if we are at the Judgment Seat and not at the White Throne Judgment, so we are home free.

I know that I am trivializing a theological debate that has gone on among Baptists for years about the nature of the judgment. I remember an incident that happened while I was the song leader for our church in Ohio. The song, "There's a Great Day Coming," seemed appropriate to a particular service. When I suggested this to the pastor while we were preparing the order of service, he looked at me like I was an atheist. "Brother Paul, we can't sing that song," he said. "It is unscriptural. It speaks of a general judgment."

I looked closely at the words of the song and, sure enough, they said that "the saints and the sinners will be parted right and left." I wondered aloud where the songwriter got such a preposterous idea. I suggested that maybe those words were straight from Jesus' mouth to

Matthew's pen, but all I got was a lecture about "rightly dividing the Word of truth," and taking things out of context.

The reason I am trivializing this debate is because it is trivial; the central issue is not the color of the throne, whether there will be one judgment or two judgments, or if there are two judgments, whether they are a thousand years apart.

Who cares? What difference does it make? The central issue is that we are all going to stand before Jesus in judgment, and each of us will be asked some very important questions, assuming Jesus knew what he was talking about in Matthew 25.

Jesus said that he, himself, will sit on a glorious throne with all nations gathered before him. He said that all of us will be divided into two groups based on the answers that our lives provide to some very tough questions. He indicated in another discourse that some very religious people will end up on his bad side, even some preachers, prophets, miracle workers, and those who have cast out devils in his name.

As Baptists, we do not even need to look into the Bible to know what the questions are, do we? They are so obvious. The questions have to be: Did you accept Jesus as your personal Savior? Do you know the day and the hour it occurred? Have you been baptized by immersion? Are you active in a Bible-believing church? Do you read the Bible and pray daily? Do you tithe? Are you a soul winner?

As strange as it may seem, if we want to go by what Jesus said, none of these sacred Baptist questions will be asked at the judgment. That hurts! Our whole Baptist definition of Christian maturity is wrapped up in these questions. What else is there? What else could there be?

The questions that we must answer at the judgment will relate to how we treated Jesus. I know that it sounds like Baptist heresy, but the mere words, "I accepted him as my personal Savior," do not appear to suffice.

The questions go much deeper than saying the right words. The questions go to the heart of who Jesus is and what he expects of those of us who say that we have a relationship with him. He made it clear that our relationship with other people is synonymous with our relationship with him. Our treatment of the weakest, the poorest, and the most defenseless is what he measures as our treatment of him. I am afraid that many of us are rocking along, living lives that are morally acceptable in the eyes of most other people, depending on what has been called "cheap grace," but totally ignorant of what Jesus expects of us.

Jesus said that those who will inherit the Kingdom are those who fed him when he was hungry, gave him drink when he was thirsty, provided hospitality to him when he was a stranger, clothed him when he was naked, and visited him when he was sick and in prison. Let us not miss the meaning of this. Jesus said that those who will spend eternity with him will be those who have fed the hungry, provided drink for the thirsty, provided hospitality to the stranger, provided clothing for those needing it, and ministered to the sick and imprisoned.

How does this square with the Baptist teaching of "grace alone?" It sounds like Jesus was teaching a "works" theology. How do we get back to those good, safe, Baptist maturity questions and leave the mysteries of Jesus' "hard teaching" to eternity?

I do not think there is any question but that many of us Baptists have bought into the "cheap grace" belief. We believe that we make a decision to receive Christ by going forward in a church service, praying the sinner's prayer, following the Roman road—or some other equally acceptable Baptist method which leads to our making a public profession of faith—being baptized, and joining the church. Then we are sealed for heaven.

Once this is done, we can go on with our lives, relatively unencumbered by the demands of the Christian faith, going through the Baptist ritual when we feel like it, but assured that, regardless of the life that we live, we will go to heaven when we die. What looms so ominously for us in the future, though, is that Jesus may have another idea, and he will be the one sitting on the throne and asking the questions.

Jesus talked a whole lot more about what he wants us to be doing here on earth than he did about getting us into heaven. Strangely, we often pay little attention to what we do here on earth; the reason that we become Christians is so we can go to heaven.

But Jesus said that he expects our acceptance of him to make a major difference in the way we relate to other people. He expects us to be entirely new creatures. I am afraid that no one has adequately explained Baptist "cheap grace" to him.

He actually expects us to treat people whom we may deem to be the "scum of the earth" just as if they were he. And, if we do not, he says that he will tell us to depart from him into eternal fire. This is not the judgment that I remember the evangelist describing.

Can you close your eyes and imagine what the final judgment will be like? The sheer drama of the situation just completely overshadows any other event that the human mind has ever dreamed. I think that the single most interesting moment will be when Pontius Pilate stands before Christ in a reversal of their earthly roles. That will be the ultimate irony.

Wouldn't you hate to be the person in line behind the Apostle Paul at the judgment? After Paul rattles off the events of his life, how he gave up home, family, and personal gain for the gospel; how he traveled across much of the known world to preach the gospel; and how he was imprisoned, beaten, stoned, shipwrecked, snake bitten, and then, for his finale, beheaded for the gospel, how weak will my pitiful testimony sound?

How do you think Adolph Hitler will answer Jesus' questions about his murder of millions of God's chosen people?

Can you picture the medieval church leader beginning his testimony proudly by telling Jesus how diligent he had been in his defense of the Bible? His most righteous moment, he might relate, was when he and others tortured Galileo to force him to recant his belief in the atheistic teachings of Copernicus about the earth revolving around the sun. And then imagine the look on his face when Jesus tells him that, in fact, the earth does [or did] revolve around the sun.

It will be interesting to hear the explanations of some of the media evangelists of our day. I wonder how they will try to justify their opulent, self-indulgent lifestyles, their dishonest money-raising methods, their fake healings, and other evidences of their lack of concern for the ones to whom they claim to be ministering. I think some of them will be surprised to be there and find out that God actually exists. If they even suspected that God was real, surely they would not be so foolish as to pretend to be doing those things in God's name and think that he would not judge them.

What about the prominent Baptist who is told by Jesus that "I needed a good education when I was a little child and you prevented me from getting it"? "You must have me confused with someone else," the Baptist will respond. "I worked untiringly for education. Why, I was a leader in the building of a Christian school at our Baptist church." Jesus might respond, "You denied me an education when you built a school in my name so your children would not have to go to school with me," and when you joined the efforts to deny funding of the public school that I attended with so many of my little brothers and sisters."

I am sure that some of us will hear him say, "I had AIDS and you abandoned me." Or, "I had AIDS and you ignored me." Or, "I had AIDS and you ridiculed me."

My son, Mike, attended Southeastern Baptist Theological Seminary for one semester. This was during the time of great turmoil at Southeastern; and when most of the professors whom Mike admired were forced to leave, Mike left, too.

Mike told me that while he was at Southeastern, he did preach one sermon. He said that it was in his Christian ethics class and that he brought up the subject of AIDS and how Baptists could and should minister to those suffering from the disease. "AIDS! Puh-leez"; "that's been done to death"; and "those people are being punished for their sin, anyway"—these responses showed the general tone of the seemingly unanimous reactions that he received from his classmates, future Baptist pastors and leaders.

"I used the story of the Good Samaritan as my text and I preached to that class for forty-five minutes," Mike told me. "After the class, the professor asked me to stay for awhile so we could talk. The professor cried as he told me that he had a close friend who had just died of AIDS and that he had been afraid to tell anyone about it."

What does the term "perseverance of the saints" mean to you? This is an old term, probably from Calvinism, that gets us pretty close to Jesus' teachings about being ready for the judgment. It relates our Christian lives to our commitment to Christ.

My mother, raised in a devout Methodist home in the early 1900s, had a clear understanding of what "perseverance of the saints" meant to the Methodists of her day. Although she was a Baptist for the last sixty years of her life, she never completely let go of her belief that "saints *must* persevere or they are no longer saints." This meant to Mom that a Christian must strive to live a holy life, an unselfish life, a life devoted to God and others. She was the person best prepared for the judgment whom I ever knew, even though her theology leaned slightly toward works in order to retain salvation.

My father, a staunch Baptist, had his equally clear understanding of "perseverance of the saints." He would have agreed, basically, with theologian Dale Moody. Dad believed that "saints *will* persevere or they were never saints in the first place."

This meant to Dad that a person truly born of God, by virtue of a new nature, will live an unselfish life devoted to God and others. Stated conversely, this means that the person who does not persevere is not born of God. Baptist theology can be tough.

Either way I cut it, I am stuck with a principle that was ingrained in me by both parents: being a Christian has to make a difference in my life. Otherwise, I am just kidding myself about my relationship to God, and I am just going through the motions of religious ritual.

In Luke 9 we read about three men who said that they wanted to follow Jesus "wherever you go." But, when faced with the realities of true discipleship, they were not willing to accept the life that Jesus had in store for them as his disciples. They all apparently had something else to do, or other relationships that had higher priority, or other excuses that prevented them from living up to their words of commitment.

I have known, as I am sure you have, some people who went through the Baptist salvation ritual. Then they lived lives that gave no evidence whatsoever of repentance, conversion, new birth, or the presence of the Holy Spirit.

I remember attending the funeral of a man who had lived a life of drunken debauchery, neglected his family, abused his wife, and, from all appearances, totally wasted his life in selfish pursuits. His funeral was conducted by a preacher who recalled a time, many years before, when the deceased had walked down the aisle of a Baptist church and professed that he had accepted Christ. Based on that one act, we were assured that the departed one was now "at rest, in heaven, and being comforted in the arms of Jesus."

Maybe the preacher was right. I have not been given the job of pronouncing judgment on anyone; that is a job that Jesus reserved for himself. But that kind of a life does not sound like what Jesus said he will be looking for at the judgment.

It is not my intention to make any reader nervous about whether old Uncle Henry or Aunt Sadie did, or did not, make it through the Pearly Gates. That is entirely up to the judgment of a holy and sovereign God. It is my sole intention to cause two people, you and me, to consider our lives in comparison to the expectations expressed by our Lord and Savior.

The parable that Jesus told about the farmer sowing seed, as recorded in Matthew 13, gives us more insight into Jesus' teachings and his expectations of us. The seed was sown, a lot of it sprouted, but only some of it bore fruit. Jesus said that this parable represented the spreading of the Word and our reception of the Word.

Some people are like a heavily worn, compacted roadbed and are so impervious to the Word that they do not even let the seed sprout. Some of us let the Word "sprout," but it quickly fades and wilts because there is no depth to our commitment. Some of us let the word "sprout," but then permit it to become entangled with things of this world and remain unfruitful. Some, thank God, let his Word "sprout" in our lives and grow on to maturity and produce fruit, "some a hundredfold."

Now, which of the persons represented in this parable will be ready for the judgment? I will not try to draw hard and fast lines regarding which of the people in this story are saved and which ones are lost. I do, however, challenge you to study this parable along with Jesus' description of the judgment.

I hope you will agree that the parable provides a pretty clear description of "persevering saints." I also believe that our Baptist theology on the subject should teach us that, as new creations in Christ Jesus, we must be, like Paul, "constrained by the love of Christ," to persevere. If we are not, I fear that many of us will hear, "Depart from me. I never knew you." Remember, Jesus said that a lot of religious people are going to receive that terrifying, devastating message.

Jesus' parable does not indicate to me that we accept salvation and then lose it, but rather that when we are so callous, shallow, or entangled with the world, we never actually accept it. I think my parents were right. Saints will/must persevere.

Sometimes I wonder if we would have so many "fading sprouts" and "entangled sprouts" in our Baptist experience if, rather than only emphasizing the need for people to become believers in Christ, we would emphasize the need for people to become followers of Christ.

Being a follower rather than just a believer fits in pretty well with James' admonition, "Be ye doers of the word and not hearers only, deceiving your own selves." How many of us are "hearers only," and thereby are deceiving ourselves into thinking that we are ready for the judgment? If God's people who are called Baptists would get ready for the judgment, what difference would it make in the world? What does Jesus expect of us? He expects us to feed the hungry.

The request that we make when we pray the Lord's Prayer, to "give us this day our daily bread," has been granted to those of us now living in the United States to a greater extent than at any other time in history or any other place in the world. We are so well fed that we take our daily bread for granted. Many of us living in the United States spend more money in a month on schemes to help us lose excess weight than most people in the world have to spend on food for a year.

I have a scenario in my mind for a television spot which would go something like this: An alien being approaches an American who is standing in the front yard of his or her large home with two luxury cars in the driveway. "I am here to grant you one wish," the visitor would say. "What is your wish?" The American quickly looks around and responds, "I want a larger house," or, "I want another car."

The scene then shifts, and the visitor approaches a mother in one of the less fortunate portions of the world with the same question. "I am here to grant you one wish," the visitor announces. "What is your wish?" The answer is instant: "I wish for enough food to feed my family today," she replies. That mother's wish would be the number-one wish for a majority of people now living in the world: "I wish for enough food to feed my family today."

We are in a position to take this portion of the Lord's Prayer for granted, while there are millions of people who go to bed hungry every night and each day hundreds or even thousands actually die due to hunger and malnutrition. Can you imagine getting up every day of your life with your first overwhelming, frightening thought being, "How will I feed my family today"? If we are serious about getting ready for the judgment, we need to feed the hungry, just as if each hungry person was Jesus, himself; thus, most of us should eat less and share more.

Do you remember what Jesus said about sharing our food in Luke 14:13-14? He said, "When you give a dinner, invite the poor, the crippled, the lame, the blind, . . . for you will be repaid at the resurrection of the righteous." Some of us need to adopt a less extravagant lifestyle so we can have more to share. Others of us need to use less resources so they can be used by others.

All of us need to give time, money, and food to support local efforts such as food pantries in our churches, food banks, rescue missions, the Salvation Army, and other methods that God is using to feed the hungry. If we really see Jesus in the ranks of the hungry in our community, we will do our best to feed him.

We need to make an impact on world hunger. We can do this individually by giving money to any of a number of trustworthy

organizations that direct their efforts to the starving and malnour-
ished people of the world.

We may have an opportunity to influence the way our church's
money is spent to assure that some of it helps to feed the hungry.
Wouldn't it be ironic if the church, the bride of Christ itself, was negli-
gent in carrying out the wish of the Bridegroom to feed the hungry?

We also need to look at how we, as a society, are spending our
nation's resources as we bask in our role as the sole "superpower" on
earth. Does the warning "to whom much is given, much will be
required" mean anything to us in our privileged situation?

Are we, as a society, truly interested in relieving the suffering of the
people Jesus identifies with, or are we more interested in maintaining
our standard of living? I have discussed this with some very religious
people in high places in our government and have gotten some strange
answers. I have been told that we should not feed the hungry children
of Ethiopia because they will grow up to be Communists and, thus, our
enemies.

I have been told that the suffering of the poor of the world is God's
punishment on them for rejecting him, and we should not interfere. I
do not buy these or similar arguments. Jesus is out there in all societies and situations, and he is hungry. Sometimes, he is starving. Will
we feed him or not? This question should influence how, and for whom,
we vote and the public policies that we support.

Jesus fed the hungry when he was on earth. Now, he expects us, as
his followers and emulators, to do the same.

Jesus stated we would do greater things than he had done. How can
this be? At this time and place in history, we have the necessary
wealth, technology, and natural resources to eliminate hunger from the
world. If Baptists got serious about this subject, there are enough of us
to start a movement that would "turn the world upside down." And is
that not what his disciples are supposed to do?

Similarly, we could have great impacts on the massive needs for
adequate, safe water for the people of the world who are thirsty. Our
involvement may be as simple as helping one family get a safe well. Or,
it might involve supporting a low-income community in its efforts to get
included on a public water system. Or, it might be as complex as
helping a struggling country combat desertification.

If we really got down to business doing what Jesus wants us to, we
could actually provide enough clothing to keep the needy warm

through the winter. We could join Jimmy Carter in helping to provide housing for the homeless.

If we followed Christ's instructions and the leading of the Holy Spirit, we would eliminate all the loneliness that exists in our nursing homes and hospitals. If significant numbers of Baptists started visiting people in jail, our country could begin to experience true prisoner rehabilitation and true prison reform resulting just from our love, concern, and involvement.

Why, if we only got started, maybe there would not be a shortage of potential foster parents or adoptive parents for hard-to-place children. There would never be a shortage of blood donors.

Who knows what great things God could do through us? Is it possible that through us, all people could be blessed? Now, let me ask you the same question that my grandfather asked Mr. Smith so many years ago: "Are you ready for the judgment?"

3 . . . Would Repent of the Sin of Racism

SOCIETY CONSIDERS ME TO BE CAUCASIAN, OR "WHITE." MY mother used to talk about her little dark-skinned grandmother who was one-half American Indian, or "red." This means that I am of mixed ancestry, but nobody cares. The white "majority" society has decided that I am one of them. One of the evidences of the persistence of racism in our society is that, if I were one-sixteenth African-American instead of American Indian, I would not be considered "white" by the "majority" society.

A few years ago, while I was working with Marie Reynolds, an African-American woman, in planning a work force diversity conference, we discovered that we had something in common. We both had American Indian ancestors. However, we were not considered to be "Euroindian" and "Afroindian." Neither were we considered to be two multiracial people. We were viewed by society to be a white man and a black woman. Our mixed ancestries did not receive any consideration.

There are no little boxes on surveys to indicate "mixed ancestry." We are slaves—pun intended—to the designation that the "majority" society puts on us; that means if even the smallest fraction of our ancestry is African-American, then we are told to mark "black" as our race.

I am told to mark "white," which means that my American Indian ancestry does not matter to our society. I would also be considered white if a fraction of my ancestry was Asian. But, let me reiterate, If my ancestry was one-sixteenth African-American instead of American Indian, I would not be white; I would be told that I am black.

32

I am belaboring this point, not to indicate that there is anything wrong with being black. Far from it. If I were one-sixteenth African-American, I would proudly put my mark in the "black" box. My point is that we, as a society, continue to put a unique stigma on African-American ancestry, and it is still treated as something that must be traced and identified as if there is something wrong with it. By so doing, we are saying to people with mixed ancestry, "We are only interested in the side of your ancestry that we, the majority, consider important. We will decide which side that is and categorize you."

I am sure that most people are like me and are proud of all sides of their heritages, not just the one that our society wants to keep track of. How about one box for race marked "human race?" If not, then how about one for multiracial? If that is unacceptable, then let us develop some new little boxes for all of us: Indoeuropean, Afroeuropean, Indoafroeuropean, Afroindoeuroasian, etc.

I started getting my inspiration for this book all the way back in the 1950s and 1960s during the height of the civil rights movement. Day after day, on the news, I saw Baptists protesting racist laws and unequal treatment. I also saw Baptist law enforcement officers using clubs, high pressure water hoses, and attack dogs as they harassed and arrested the protesting Baptists. I heard of Baptist prisoners holding prayer meetings in jail where they were ridiculed by Baptist jailers. I even harbored the horrible thought that maybe some Baptist was involved in the bombing murder of those little girls in their Sunday School class in a Baptist church.

The civil rights movement came to be led by Martin Luther King Jr., a Baptist minister. Most of his inner circle of close associates were also Baptists.

King led a campaign to achieve equality that was based on Christian principles and behavior; yet many Baptist congregations were being told by their ministers that "Martin Lucifer Koon is not of God," and must be opposed. And King countered: "If we are wrong, God Almighty is wrong. If we are wrong, justice is a lie." That was when the obvious hit me squarely between the eyes; something was terribly, terribly wrong with God's people who call ourselves Baptists.

I was raised as a Baptist in a racially segregated society that I did not seriously question until my late teens. I can recall hearing the opinions of one visiting relative, a Baptist, of course, that the KKK was made up of good Christian people, that black people did not possess souls, that race war was inevitable, and all sorts of other garbage. I am thankful that this was not the everyday atmosphere in our home when I was a child, but I was taught that racial separation was the way that God wanted it.

I remember extremely well the day of the Supreme Court decision in 1954, Brown vs. the Board of Education, which ruled that school segregation was unconstitutional. I was a sophomore in high school, and the first people with whom I discussed it were two teachers who saw nothing but Communism and future bloodshed in the decision. In fact, I only recall one teacher at Talcott High School, Robert E. Via, who defended the Court's decision and told us that this was long overdue.

I do not remember a single Baptist preacher or other Baptist leader in our area who spoke in favor of the ruling. I do, however, recall powerful statements about the forces that were at work to disrupt "God's holy order" of things.

Desegregation did not come during my remaining two years of high school, and I left for college in the fall of 1956, still without experiencing any semblance of an integrated society. I went to college at West Virginia University, where I first sat in the classroom with African-Americans.

Old WVU was not, however, a liberal outpost in a racist environment. The mighty Mountaineers, who lost the NCAA basketball championship by one measly point to the University of California in 1959, had an all-white team. WVU did not begin to integrate its sports program until after my graduation in 1960.

I did learn a lot about equality in college, though. I took courses with African-Americans who were smarter than I was. I played basketball against some African-Americans who demonstrated, very convincingly, that some of them were more physically skilled than I was, too. College provided me with the first opportunity that I had ever had to get to know African-Americans of my age and come to an awareness that they had interests and ambitions that were similar to my own. My eyes began to open.

My great moment of truth came as the result of a class assignment while I was at WVU. Looking back, I can see that God used something as mundane as a social science class to give me insight into his will. One of the requirements in the class was to do some type of community service. One of the options was an outreach program of the Methodist Church in Morgantown. That sounded like working in a Baptist church, almost, so that was the one that I chose.

My assignment was to go out to a nearby coal-mining community and assist a church employee who managed a church-owned roller-skating rink. The church had bought and converted an abandoned building into the roller rink for the use of the kids who lived there. Duck Soup! I liked roller skating and I liked kids. What a snap! This was going to be the easiest and most enjoyable assignment of the semester.

When I got there I found that all the kids were African-American. No big deal, I thought. Kids are kids. The kids started out a little stand-offish toward me, but as the day wore on, we started getting acquainted. My main task was helping the kids get their skates on properly. This involved my kneeling down at their feet and serving them. This symbolism struck me immediately. It is remarkable how God can teach us so much more when we are on our knees than when we are "standing tall."

As the kids became more comfortable with me, they really opened up. They wanted to know who I was and if I was "the preacher." They began talking openly to me about their hopes and dreams. I listened as one after another predicted perfect futures for themselves. They were going to be rich, successful, major league, world conquerors.

All this was familiar because they had not thought of a thing for themselves that I had not dreamed of for myself. I had reached the age at which I was analyzing just which of my childhood dreams could possibly still come true and which ones I would have to abandon. Through this prism of self-analysis, I tried to evaluate their chances of realizing any of their dreams.

Some of the kids had severe physical problems. I attributed the misshapen legs to earlier bouts with rickets. Extremely thick glasses indicated vision impairment. A few of the kids were unusually small and frail for their age.

Most of the kids had communication problems. I could hardly understand what some of them were saying due to their speech impediments. They all spoke in a heavy ethnic idiom, for which they would someday be penalized by the "majority" culture.

My last assignment, after helping to remove the skates and being repeatedly told "goodbye" by every one of the kids, was to drive a carload of them to their homes. Here God finished the picture for me.

I was not prepared for the emotion that welled up inside me as I piled eight or ten of those little children into my ancient Buick and took them, one by one, to their homes. To say that their homes were modest would be an understatement. Yet, in the front of every home was a mother, sometimes a father, and often a yard full of brothers and sisters eagerly awaiting the child.

This was the first time that I truly saw myself in the people that I had been taught were so different from me. I began to see myself in the joys, hopes, and ambitions that the children had shared with me at the roller rink. But now, as I identified fully with the love that I saw being expressed between mother and child, father and child, and between brothers and sisters, I think I felt like Peter must have felt when God got his attention and showed him that he is "not a respecter of persons." In his sight, we are all the same.

As I started to comprehend this great truth, the troubled feelings that I had experienced as I had listened to the dreams of those children developed into deep frustration. What chance will they have in a world that will automatically penalize them because of their skin color?

Add to this the fact that some of them have physical conditions and other limitations that will probably go uncorrected. And then add to these the other results of poverty, cultural deprivation, etc., and then calculate the chances of just one of them reaching the first step of the heights to which they all now naively aspire.

That day, on my drive back to the campus, I repented of the sin of racism. Since then, my life has never been the same.

To the Baptist who says, "I am not racist and I have nothing to repent for," let me say two things: first, I do not believe you; and second, you are a part of a group, Baptists, that has a lot to repent for.

To the Baptist who says, "I was not there when it happened. I am not responsible for the actions of others, even if they were Baptists," let me point out something. Every Easter we are moved by the song, "Were You There When They Crucified My Lord?" We sit in the pew and, as we listen to the song and reflect on it, tears well up in our eyes; and we whisper "Amen" as we acknowledge that, yes, we were there when that great injustice was done. We were a part of it just as if we had been there.

If we can see ourselves in the corporate sins that resulted in the crucifixion of Christ two thousand years ago, surely it is not too big a stretch for us to see ourselves in the corporate sins of injustice that are now being committed, or have been committed in the short lifetime of our country. I pray that you will permit God to open your eyes and help you to deal with this sin. If you do, he will give you the peace that comes when you see things as he sees them and when you repent and surrender to his will.

Now I am going to make a major point. If God's people who are called Baptists had let the Holy Spirit lead in their actions, the civil rights movement would not have been a time of anger and violence; it would have been a time of spiritual revival.

Let me say that again! If God's people who are called Baptists had let the Holy Spirit lead in their actions, the civil rights movement would not have been a time of anger and violence; it would have been a time of spiritual revival. Sure, there would still have been a social upheaval, but is that not what the result should be when a sinful situation is confronted by the power of the gospel of Jesus Christ?

Can you imagine what kind of "Crusades for Christ" there could have been if, instead of turning to traditional wisdom—prejudice— white Baptists had united with each other and with black Baptists to seek God's will through Bible study and prayer? Just think about the potential of the two Baptist giants of our time, Billy Graham and Martin Luther King Jr., combining their charismatic skills, with our support, to conduct crusades to spread the saving and liberating gospel of Christ. Think of the spiritual impact that would have been achieved by such crusades as a united effort of millions of Baptists and thousands of Baptist churches throughout the country.

Think of the church growth that would have occurred. Think of the new churches that would have been established. Think of the example that we would have been to all of Christianity and to the whole world.

Think of the young people who would have been saved if they had seen a group of Christians who followed Christ and reached out to them with the gospel, instead of retreating into their prejudices and fighting to preserve their sinful condition. Think of the young black people who grew up in Baptist families who would still be Baptist if they had seen hope in the church of their parents.

Instead of chasing away these young people to Islam, Jehovah's Witnesses, or other religions that recruited them by offering them full acceptance and answers to some of their problems, Baptists could have provided acceptance and answers relating to unemployment, lack of needed skills, low self-esteem, and endless other problems which have resulted from our selfish neglect. I think that God will judge us for not offering the hope, equal acceptance, moral discipline, and spiritual guidance that these young people were seeking and had to find in other religions.

Think of the young white people who grew up in Baptist families who would still be active Baptists if they had not seen hypocrisy in the church of their parents. One particular event which happened in the early 1970s while I was living in Florida stands out in my mind. A young man in the First Baptist Church felt that God was calling him to preach while he was still in high school. He shared this with a small group of his friends at church and then, with the blessing of the church, he and his friends initiated some evangelistic efforts aimed at the youth of the community.

Their efforts were spectacular. They found that the young people were hungry for the gospel and many were being saved. The members of the First Baptist Church were so happy with the turn of events that they rented a building and established a Christian coffeehouse for the young people to use as a center for their activities. One of their most successful functions was to attract a crowd of young people to the coffeehouse on Saturday nights, where the young evangelist and his friends would present the gospel. One of their best attractions was the use of local Christian young people to provide music and testimonies.

The high school prom queen was a devout Baptist. She was also a terrific singer. It therefore seemed reasonable for the young evangelist and his group to invite this young woman to sing and give her testimony at the coffeehouse on Saturday night—reasonable to the young people, maybe, but not to the pastor and deacon board of the First Baptist Church, because the young woman was African-American.

As soon as the pastor heard of the situation, he called an emergency meeting of the deacon board on Friday night. They voted to immediately close the coffeehouse so the scheduled Saturday night event could not take place.

I do not know what happened to the young evangelist, but I was acquainted with the family of another very active young man in the group. That young man became so disillusioned with the action of the deacons that he openly questioned whether there were any saved people in the entire church, especially the pastor and deacons. He even challenged the validity of his father's faith, although his father, a deacon, had voted against closing the coffeehouse.

I have not had any recent contact with that young man's family. The last I heard from them, the young man had dropped out of a Baptist college and was no longer active in any church.

Just imagine the potential organizational and political skills that would have been brought to bear on the greatest social issue of our generation if leaders like Jesse Jackson and Jerry Falwell had sought common ground in the gospel of Christ and worked together to bring about the salvation of our people and our society.

The list of combinations of Baptist leaders could go on and on. One that particularly intrigues me would be Ralph David Abernathy and W. A. Criswell. You can add to this list, hopefully including the pastors of the First Baptist Church and the largest predominantly black Baptist church in your own community.

But it did not happen. Opportunity was lost. Remember the words of John Greenleaf Whittier: "For of all sad words of tongue or pen, the saddest are these: It might have been!"

Just what did we, as white Baptists, do when the injustice of racism became the overwhelming issue of the day and God needed us to take the lead in showing his nature and will? We stood on the sidelines and watched as the major political parties debated the issue and began to develop new, fairer positions for their platforms. We stuck our heads in the sand as other denominations began to move in the direction of equality for all.

Some white Baptists undoubtedly began to do some soul searching, but, by and large, we sat in the back row of American society, searching the Bible to find support for our prejudiced opinions. And, boy, did we find them. "Be not unequally yoked together" was the indignant response that I received from my pastor in Ohio, in the mid-1960s, when I challenged him to scripturally defend his racist diatribes. "All of this will lead to intermarriage, and God says that is a terrible sin," he concluded.

When I pointed out what the preacher already knew, that the unequal yoking had to do with marriage between believers and unbelievers, marriages which he performed regularly, he realized that he had just run out of proof texts. He then weakly rationalized racism, based on his own prejudice, and demonstrated his total lack of knowledge about the subject of civil rights.

"The great sin of intermarriage" has been widely assumed to be the ultimate debate closer by racist Baptists. Once the discussion gets seriously heated, the invoking of intermarriage, usually by using the words "how would you like for your sister to marry one?" is meant to strike a fatal fear in the mind of any "misguided" Baptist.

Two very effective responses to the "ultimate" question about my position on intermarriage have come to me in different ways. First, I discovered that Moses, himself, the law giver, married an Ethiopian woman. I have found that most people pontificating on intermarriage do not know that. Once that fact is established, the obvious follow-up question is, "How did God react to this intermarriage?"

I have always used the Bible to show the answer. It is truly amazing to see someone discover for the first time, from God's Word, that God afflicted Moses' sister Miriam with leprosy because she spoke against Moses' marriage. Hot Flash! God did not punish the person who inter-married; he punished the person who opposed it!

Second, in response to "how would you like for your sister to marry one?" I have been able to say for the past thirty-some years, "She did!" That is to say, my sister-in-law did.

Judy, my wife's youngest sister, seemingly lost all interest in boys during her late teen years. When she dated a young man, it appeared to be emotionless; she often seemed to prefer just to go out with one or two of her girl friends. Then, when she was about nineteen or twenty, while visiting Rose and me, she shared her secret with us.

Judy had been secretly dating Gerald, an African-American, with whom she had fallen in love and planned to marry. They knew that such a marriage was illegal in West Virginia, so they were making plans to slip away to Massachusetts to be married. This they promptly did.

Talk about turmoil in a household! Initially, Rose and I were the only ones in the family who were not devastated by Judy's and Gerald's marriage, and no one in the family wanted to hear our points of view. Rose's dad, mom, brother, sister, aunts, uncles, cousins, in-laws, and out-laws were angry, disappointed, and embarrassed by Judy's action.

It has been enlightening, but painful, to be a part of a family's forced awakening to the evils of racism. I have been particularly intrigued by the process that my father-in-law has gone through. Soon after the news of Judy and Gerald hit in his community, my father-in-law abruptly stopped going out to Bruce's, a local gathering spot where, for years, he had joined his friends on Friday evenings after his week's work on the C&O Railroad.

I got some insight into how he was being treated by his former friends one day as he and I were standing in his front yard a hundred feet or so from the highway. An old Chevy pickup, struggling to reach the top of Tunnel Hill just past my father-in-law's house, was chugging along at about fifteen miles an hour as the driver stuck his head out the window and yelled, "Hey, Coon!"

My father-in-law, always a proud man, did not look up or respond. He just began a deliberate retreat into his house. His reaction, or lack of one, told me that this type of harassment was a common occurrence.

My father-in-law's anger against Judy and Gerald seemingly consumed him. Although he rejected the advice of one of his own brothers to kill Gerald, he rarely referred to Gerald; when he did, he spoke angrily, using a racial epithet. When Judy brought her first child, Tommy, to visit his grandparents, my father-in-law refused to have any contact with, or even to look at, his grandchild.

Tommy died a few weeks later of Sudden Infant Death Syndrome. The first time Grandpa looked at his grandson was after he had died. The first time that Gerald and Judy were together in the presence of Judy's family was at the funeral home. The first time that Judy's family and Gerald's family had ever been in the same room was at the funeral home.

When Robin, Judy's and Gerald's second child, was born and brought to her grandparent's house for a visit, her Grandpa was there to greet her. It was the same for Jerome and Tonya when they came along. Change had taken place and continued to take place. As years passed, even Gerald was accepted by his father-in-law as, gradually, reason replaced prejudice and truth triumphed over the ugly falsehood of racism.

At a Fourth of July celebration in Alderson a few years ago, my family and Gerald's family were standing together as the parade passed by. Suddenly, the driver of a beautiful antique car stopped and called to Robin, now about twenty-three years old. "Are you Miss America?" he asked. "No, I'm not," Robin replied, looking embarrassed, but flattered. "Well, you should be!" was the driver's comment as he drove away to rejoin the parade.

Later that day, I related that story to my father-in-law as our families sat on his front porch and he was sitting in the swing beside Robin. We then began to question Robin as to her love life, pointing out that at twenty-three she was virtually an old maid and that she should make her move while she still had her looks.

Finally, to shut us up, Robin admitted that there was someone very special in her life back home in Massachusetts. "Is he black or white?"

was Grandpa's question. "He's black, Grandpa," Robin responded. "Well, I was hoping that while you were here, you'd find yourself a white feller," Grandpa said, impishly.

That moment of hilarity broke up the crowd and they scattered, leaving just my father-in-law and me on the porch. "We've come a long way, haven't we, Grandpa," I said, after we had sat in silence for a few minutes. "What do you mean?" he asked.

"I seem to recall that some of us weren't too happy about things when Judy married Gerald," I reminded him. "But here twenty some years later, you are able to sit with your black-and-white family and joke with your granddaughter about the color of her boyfriend." As the conversation went on between us, the man who had once refused to even acknowledge the existence of his own grandson agreed that God had been good to us and we had been blessed by having a mixed marriage in our family.

If every family had experienced the growth that our family had experienced and if everyone knew what we now knew, we agreed, the problem of racism would be solved. Think of how much heartache and suffering we all would have avoided and the blessing we would have been to the world if white Baptists had repented of the sin of racism when we were confronted with it by our black Baptist brothers and sisters in the 1950s and 1960s.

In the very same way that our family experienced so much pain and missed so much joy because of prejudice, Baptist churches have paid a great price for their disobedience. One of the greatest prices that we have paid is that the opportunity that we had to lead our society out of this terrible sin has been lost.

There were so many of us Baptists, black and white, located so close together, worshipping the same God, and claiming the same Christ. But instead of coming together to spread and live out the gospel, we often ended up fighting each other. I really doubt that God is pleased with us. Let's face it! We Baptists were the answer to the civil rights problem in the United States and we blew it! I think that calls for some repenting, don't you?

Now here is another "biggie" that I want you to read twice and think about for a long time. Have you ever considered that Baptists could have, and should have, prevented the Civil War?

If just the Baptists in this country in the first half of the nineteenth century had taken God seriously, recognizing that in Christ there is no free nor slave, and that he is no respecter of persons, their actions and influence would have revolutionized the society without a fight. Baptist plantation owners would have freed their slaves and helped them become established as free people. Baptist preachers would have "rightly divided the Word" and encouraged the practice of equality and the golden rule.

But this did not happen. Instead, plantation owners became more and more militant in their defense of their right to own human beings as farm animals.

And guess who helped them in this defense? That's right! As unbelievable as it seems, the good old Baptist preacher was standing with them, telling them that they were preserving God's holy order for the family and society. "Slaves, obey your masters" became a most popular text for the Baptist sermons in the mid-1800s in churches in slaveholding areas as the controversy over slavery heated to a fever pitch.

"God's holy order begins with the man's authority over his wife, then over his children, and then over his slaves," many Baptist congregations were assured. "Any person or any government that tries to change this order of things is going against the teaching of God and is sure to fail."

Of course, not all Baptists felt this way. Some were strong abolitionists at that time. The debates that raged over slavery between the Baptist factions at the national level led to the splitting of the largest body of Baptists into two denominations, Northern Baptists (now American Baptist) and Southern Baptists.

Some diehard Southern Baptists still insist that slavery had absolutely nothing to do with the great Baptist split; it was all over a disagreement about missions. Right! Sure!

The fact that the split occurred just before the outbreak of the Civil War, that the lines of demarcation were the same lines that were soon to define the Confederacy, and that slavery was the overwhelmingly consuming issue of the time—was all of this mere coincidence? Anyone who would buy that would believe that the Civil War was fought over making the magnolia the national flower. Some controversy regarding missions was going on at the time, but even that discussion centered around slavery and whether slave owners were fit to be missionaries.

My guess is that those who hold that slavery had no part in the Baptist split are among those who would like to avoid the need for Baptists to acknowledge our sin and seek God's forgiveness. Often these are the same people who insist that they are not racist and therefore have nothing to repent of, either individually or corporately.

Isn't it amazing that the people whom God had in place who could have prevented the Civil War chose to split and fight each other rather than to seek God's will and work together? Sounds a lot like how we reacted to the civil rights movement, doesn't it?

Have we learned? Have we repented? Have we changed? I am afraid not. Look at us. We still fight and split over every issue that arises. We add adjectives to our names to highlight our differences. We continue to demonstrate that we still would rather have our way than come together and seek God's way.

Martin Luther King Jr. and Billy Graham have both been quoted as saying, back in the 1950s, that the time from 11:00 A.M. to 12:00 noon on Sunday was the most segregated hour of the week in America. This has changed very little in most Baptist churches since those words were first uttered.

For some reason, the discredited concept of "separate but equal" still persists in the great majority of Baptist life. We still have predominantly black Baptist churches and denominational structures and predominantly white Baptist churches and denominational structures despite the fact that such a situation is anachronistic.

Our favorite sports teams, our government, our schools, our work environment, and even our country clubs are now becoming reflections of the diversity within our culture. So, where are we, God's people on earth who are called Baptists? Once again, we are at the back of the line, pathetically following others instead of being at the head of the line setting a godly example.

I do not know just exactly how God sees his people who are called Baptists, but I do have some idea how other people see us. We are not presenting the gospel of Christ in a very appealing way when we treat those who are of our own household of faith as if they are enemies.

Do you realize how gullible we look to politicians in our country? Baptists are "easy pickings" to them. Political strategists know they can exploit many groups in our society by just hitting their "hot button." With what group does the issue of race stir political fervor? Is it the military-industrial complex? Is it the environmentalists? Is it the banking industry? Is it big oil? Is it agriculture? Is it labor unions? Of course not. It is the Religious Right.

I cannot think of a greater sin being committed by people called Christians than letting the name of Christ become linked with bigotry and hatred. And I cannot think of a greater sin being committed by his people called Baptists than getting sucked into such a mess. We should know better!

It is really embarrassing to realize that all a political hack has to do is to raise the issue of race in a political campaign, have the white candidate give just a hint of bigotry, and then know that he/she can rely on a majority of white Baptist votes and big-campaign contributions. The great irony is that we are then voting to deny or delay opportunities that may be vital for some of our black Baptist brothers and sisters.

We may simply look inept to other religious groups, but sometimes we must look like total hypocrites to the unchurched world that we are supposed to be reaching. Think of the impact we could have if we all would seek God's will and work together to accomplish his will instead of always arguing and fragmenting. Just as we could have prevented the Civil War and the civil rights crisis, we could now be solving the problems of this era, which still includes the sin of racism.

What will it take for this to happen? We have clung to the sin of racism for so long, first rationalizing it and now denying it, that it is a part of who we are, and that is a Baptist shame. The thing that we must do is repent! By this I do not mean just to be sorry and to apologize for our past sins. I mean that we, you and I, must do a complete 180-degree turn and live changed lives. That is true repentance.

One of my "unfavorite" days on the church calendar is Race Relations Sunday. This event, as I have experienced it, consists of a racially homogeneous group talking about how all our problems would be solved if we would just be more tolerant. Where in the entire Bible are we called to tolerance? We are called to love! Tolerance is, maybe, ten degrees. Love is 180! We are called to 180-degree repentance!

Tolerance indicates our willingness to put up with something that we have power over. We tolerate a wart instead of cutting it off. We may tolerate a mosquito in our bedroom rather than getting up and searching for it. Aren't you glad that Jesus did not come to the world to bring tolerance? Would tolerance have led him to die on the cross for our sins? Of course not! Only love could have been his motivation. He demands no less from us. Do not repent of the sin of racism unless you are prepared to love.

We must stop looking backward at our corrupt tradition; we must fix our eyes upon Jesus and do as he would do if he were here today.

We must reread the story of the Good Samaritan and apply it. We must initiate contact and generate joint fellowship between people and churches of all races. The Baptist World Alliance can do it. Maybe we can, too.

We must seek, invite, and otherwise encourage the attendance and membership of people of all races who desire to worship God as a part of our congregation. I believe that the folks in the American Baptist Churches are ahead of the rest of us on this issue. We are making progress in our small local Southern Baptist church, and the Baptist Convention of New York, with which we are affiliated, is a very diverse group. It can happen!

We must get off the sidelines, get our heads out of the sand, get off the back row, and let God use us to show his nature and his will. If this begins with us as individuals, and then spreads into our churches, surely even the leaders of our denominations will begin to get a vision for what God wants us to be doing in the world.

Isn't this the Baptist way? First the individual, then the church, and then the denomination. Wouldn't it be great if, for once, Baptists with various labels and ethnicities would come together in love and co-operate with each other, rather than continuing to fight and split?

Clearly, we will never, ever be the force for good in the world that God wants us to be until God's people who are called Baptists humble ourselves, pray, seek his face, and repent of the sin of racism so that he can forgive us and then, through us, heal our land.

4. ... Would Let My Women Go

NOT TOO LONG AGO, THE SCRIPTURE TEXT FOR THE SUNDAY School lesson that I was teaching was in Galatians 3, which contains that great verse describing God's model for his people: "There is neither Jew nor Greek, slave nor free, male nor female, for you are all one in Christ Jesus" (v. 28, NIV).

I broke the lesson down into three parts, Baptist that I am, and laid it out as follows:

The Jew-Greek issue—We discussed how Paul, Peter, and the other early leaders of the church had to struggle with the subject of the equality of Jews and Gentiles in God's sight. This was dealt with successfully in the first century, and we all agreed that all nationalities are free to receive God's blessings through Christ.

The slave-free issue—Our discussion centered around the evils of slavery and how this subject had been dealt with decisively in the nineteenth century in the United States. We were unanimous in our condemnation of slavery.

The male-female issue—I told the class that I believed that, since this part of the lesson had been put off until our day, it was our responsibility to deal with it. Just as the early apostles had successfully dealt with the narrowness of a gospel for Jews only, and our forefathers had successfully dealt with the myth of slavery being God's will, it was our task to deal with the second-class status of women in our world; and that needed to start in our churches. I pointed out that if this Scripture passage is true, and both ethnic bias and slavery are wrong, then sexual bias, equally as significant, has to be wrong, too.

47

As I concluded the class, I asked if there were any questions or comments. A husband and wife who were traveling through our area and visiting our church that Sunday said that, yes indeed, they did have comments.

They stated that they were Sunday School teachers in a Baptist church, that they had studied the lesson from the teacher's quarterly provided by our Sunday School Board, and that I had completely perverted the lesson. They pointed out that the lesson was not about equality or anything approaching it; the lesson was about Judaizers, and I had missed the whole point.

I was forced to admit that I had not closely followed the erudite emanations coming forth from the teachers' quarterly but that I had attempted to take the Scripture text and make it relevant to our situation and time in history. I pointed out that, with all due respect to our Sunday School Board, we weren't having much trouble around here with Judaizers lately; however, there was a lot of sexism going on, especially in our Baptist churches, and God expected us to deal with it. I did not make converts of our visitors that day.

I remember a very emotional sermon that Larry Coleman preached a few years ago. Larry began his sermon by reminiscing about his days at Southeastern Baptist Theological Seminary and recalling that he was not the top student in his class. But Larry did remember, vividly, the person who was the top student in the class. That student, according to Larry, made the best grades, was the best thinker, was the top debater, and was the most accomplished public speaker.

Following graduation, Larry and most of his fellow graduates promptly found jobs in Southern Baptist churches and began the careers for which they felt God had called them. Larry said that he kept hearing that the top student in his class was having trouble finding a job. After a period of a few years of vain searching for work in a Southern Baptist church, the student whom Larry had most admired lapsed into deep depression and committed suicide.

I am sure that you have figured out by now that this brilliant student who had surrendered to a life in the Christian ministry, but was denied it by the Baptist institution that had "raised her," was a woman. What a waste! Where is the sense in this?

Why do so many of us Baptists persist in our belief that God does not call women to his service? Or, if he does, it is only for a subservient role that is "appropriate" for a woman? This is a complete denial of

Galatians 3:28. If God does not consider women equal to men, then slavery is moral and the gospel is only for the Jews. I do not believe that God would give us Galatians 3:28 and then expect us to figure out that two-thirds of it is truth and one-third of it is a lie.

Now that I have your attention, let's look at our institutionalized, male-chauvinist, Baptist attitude and try to find our way out of the mess that we are in. At one time we did not know any better. We thought that we were just being scriptural by denying women their rightful place in the church. The passages most used by Baptists to justify the second-class status of women are in Ephesians 5–6 and Colossians 3.

These are "God's holy order" passages where wives are told to be subject to their husbands. These are also the passages which tell children to obey their parents, and slaves to be obedient to their masters.

Bear in mind that, until 1865, a majority of Baptists in the United States accepted these passages in their entirety as coming solely and directly from God. Now, even though we realize that we were dead wrong in our interpretation of these passages when we used them to justify slavery, some of us still hold tenaciously to our equally erroneous interpretations regarding the other two subjects, women and children.

Let us look at these passages and see what they say and, if possible, who said what. Paul, a man trained in Jewish rabbinical law, wrote these epistles during the time of the Roman Empire. All of the people receiving his letters were living under the rule of Roman law.

What impact did Paul's Jewish background and his awareness of Roman law have on his writings? Probably quite a bit, because one of his continuing themes was how to survive as a Christian in a world dominated by the harsh Roman government. Paul demonstrated diversity in his own behavior as he tried to balance the responsibilities of being a Christian, yet a Jew, and also a citizen of Rome.

Paul dealt in his letters to the Ephesians and Colossians with how to be a Christian in a world ruled by Roman law which was often in direct conflict with God's law. Roman law gave all power in the household to the father. Concepts like *pater familias* and *patria potestas* gave the father all of the rights in a household, even the right of life and death over his wife, his children, and his slaves.

Let's talk about the laws governing slaves and children first and then get back to the women. There were sixty million slaves in the

Roman Empire. Under Roman law the slave was a piece of property, not a person. A slave was considered an articulate animal. The only difference, in this cruel system, between a human slave and a cow was that the slave was articulate, and the cow was inarticulate. Slaves were branded and runaways could be killed on sight.

This little bit of knowledge sheds a great deal of light on the book of Philemon, which Paul wrote to a group of Christians asking them to accept Onesimus, a runaway slave, as a brother to be loved, not an animal to be killed. Remember that, in Christ, there is no difference between free and slave.

Under Roman law, the father had absolute power over his children. When a child was born, the father decided if it would live or die, or be given away to be raised as a slave or prostitute. As the child became older, the father could inflict any punishment on the child, sell the child into slavery or prostitution, or kill the child, as he saw fit. The child was never released from this cruel law, giving the father absolute power, as long as the father lived.

The wives during Paul's day were no better off than the slaves and the children. Paul had been raised and educated in the Jewish tradition that had much in common with the Roman law as it applied to wives. In both cases, the wife was the property of the husband.

In the Roman world at the time of Paul's writings, women were being married and discarded, remarried and discarded, ad infinitum, at the whims of the men. There was a complete breakdown of the family since there was no basis for home life and since fidelity of the husbands was virtually unknown.

The dilemma that Paul faced was how to help new Christians be true to God's law of equality and yet stay within the legal limits of the very ungodly Roman law of inequality which required that wives, children, and slaves be the property of the legal head of the household. Was there any way a person could be a Christian and obey these unfair and oppressive laws? There were undoubtedly many Christians who argued that they should simply ignore the Roman laws and live (or die) the consequences.

So Paul dealt with the laws one at a time. First, he quoted the Roman law that said "wives, be subject to your husbands," and then told the Christian couple how they could comply with the law. Paul simply balanced the one-sidedness of the Roman law with the fairness of God's law. Yes, the wife could be a Christian and still comply with the

Roman law by being subject to her husband, but the big news was that, as a Christian, the husband was equally responsible for the relationship. The Christian husband had to be just as committed to his wife, under God's law, as his wife was committed to him under Roman law.

Paul was brilliant! This did not violate either Caesar's law or God's law, but it would surely cut down on the divorce rate, and Christian couples would be able to show their neighbors a different type of family life. This concept of joint submissiveness fits perfectly in God's model of there being no difference between male and female.

Paul sealed his teaching on the subject by citing the example of the relationship between Christ and the church as a model husband-and-wife relationship. Similarly, Paul then told parents and children how they could be Christians and yet not violate the cruel Roman law. Again, the theme was mutual respect and dual responsibility. Paul even gave a prescription for slavery in a Christian household under Roman law, in which both the master and the slave accepted God's law of impartiality and treated each other accordingly.

Let's summarize. The three main pillars for what many Baptists have declared to be God's holy order for the family did not come from God after all. They came from Caesar, instead. Stated another way, when Baptists have used the Bible to justify putting women in a subservient status, explain away child abuse, or endorse slavery, they have not quoted God. They have quoted Caesar.

In these passages, then, we see that Paul is following the admonition of Jesus who said that we should "render unto Caesar the things that are Caesar's and unto God the things that are God's." He first quotes Caesar and then instructs the early church on how to live as Christians in a society with "unchristian" laws.

I do not know how that makes you feel, but it takes a great big load off my mind. I am excited about a biblical theology that is consistently liberating and treats everyone as equals. That is what God gave us in Galatians as his model, and I am pleased to know that there is no contradiction between what he said through Paul in Galatians and what he said, also through Paul, in Ephesians and Colossians.

Now, let me ask you, did your pastor ever tell you about *pater familias* or *patria potestas*? If not, why not?

I can understand the pastors of my childhood and youth not telling me about this. They were mostly poorly educated men who were farmers or coal miners who had felt called of God to preach. They were literally "raised up" from their local congregations and began preaching based on their experience and personal study.

What I cannot understand, though, is the reluctance of today's pastors to discuss these Roman laws. They were all taught this stuff in seminary. Yet, in my church experience, I have heard only two pastors ever mention them.

The passage most used by Baptists to justify the denial of women in the roles of pastor and deacon is 1 Timothy 3. This is the passage in which Paul discusses the traits/requirements for bishops and deacons.

Men who aspire to positions of leadership in the church are to be sober, monogamous, honest, truthful, and faithful. Then verse eleven, in the King James Version, reads as follows: "Even so must their wives be grave, not slanderers, sober, faithful in all things."

In the original Greek, the passage more correctly reads: "Even so must women deacons be grave, not slanderers, sober, faithful in all things." If you have never heard this before, it is likely that your pastor, who has studied this passage in the original Greek and knows that Paul used similar terminology for the women as he did for the men, has neglected to tell you.

What Paul did, rather than describe the traits for a leader's wife, was to give the same requirements for a female servant of God as he did for the male servant of God, with the exception of monogamy and fiscal responsibility. Paul was probably not worried about a woman having more than one husband because that was not a problem in the society at that time, and he did not worry about a woman's management of money and property, because usually she had none.

Another supporting passage which was interpreted, rather than translated, in the King James Version is Romans 16:1, which, in the original Greek, refers to Phoebe as a deacon of the church at Cenchreae. Your pastor can undoubtedly help you confirm the accuracy of the word "deacon" in that passage, too.

The King James Version of the Bible is my favorite rendering of the Scriptures. I, like many of you, was raised on this version. All of the Scripture that I have committed to memory is from the King James. This version has served well, and continues to serve well, the cause of Christ.

I believe in the inerrancy of the Scriptures, in their original form. This means that I believe that, as humans translate from the oldest known manuscripts, some interpretation creeps in. The reason your pastor had to make passing grades in Greek and Hebrew in order to graduate from seminary is because it is important for pastors to be able to study the oldest manuscripts and search for God's true message.

Consider the times of the King James Version. The English translation was commissioned by King James for use by the Church of England. The Church of England was still in its infancy, having split off from the very patriarchal Roman Catholic Church over a male-female issue, but certainly not an issue related to elevating the role of women in the church or society.

King James' grandfather, Henry the Eighth, had split with the Roman Catholic Church because the Pope would not sanction his divorce from James' grandmother, Katharine of Aragon. After establishing his new church, old grandad then proceeded to exercise his male prerogative to wed, divorce, and behead women as he saw fit.

The strong belief in the dominant role of men that existed in the Catholic Church was, thus, carried over into the Church of England and has persisted until modern times. Women were not permitted into the Anglican priesthood until the 1990s.

Against this backdrop of tradition and practice, it was politically expedient for the scholars of King James to use alternative wording to describe women who held positions in the New Testament churches. It was easier to use the word "wife" or "servant" when the text referred to a woman, and reserve the word "deacon" for masculine references, than to deal with the consequences of a more accurate translation.

Paul had two other themes regarding women that he often wrote about: their appearance and their behavior in worship services. First, let us see what he had to say about the way women looked. Paul instructed women to dress modestly and inexpensively, and not to wear jewelry. He also made a big deal about hair. He said that women should not braid it, glory in it, or leave it uncovered in a worship service. Can you imagine Paul's consternation if he were to step into a Baptist church and see the various assortments of beehives, bouffants, dreadlocks, perms, Jeri curls, French twists, and corn rows that adorn the heads of Baptist women today?

What about Paul's particular hang-ups about women's hair and the covering of women's heads? What we need to realize is that the custom of covering the face and head was, and still is, a very important part of the Middle Eastern culture. But women, set free by the power of the gospel, began to show themselves in church services without the traditional head coverings dictated by the society of their day.

In a society where a respectable woman never exposed her hair or her full face in public, a Christian woman coming to church and shedding her head covering and presenting herself bare above the neck must have been shocking and more than a little provocative. For a man who had never seen the full face and hair of a woman other than his wife or a prostitute, the event would have been, to say the least, distracting—even for a born-again, spiritual man. Do you see what Paul was up against? The contrast between the gospel and the world is sometimes very dramatic.

Second, what did Paul have to say about the behavior of women in the worship services? He wrote that women should be silent in church and not teach men. Paul may have wanted to "gradual into" the equality that he talked about in Galatians. Remember that the women were still the property of their husbands, under Roman law. Paul was very sensitive to the culture in which he and the early church lived. Living the Christian life, then even more than now, involved walking a tightrope between the freedom that they had in Christ and the constraints of their society.

Also, Paul possibly may not have been ready, personally, for the social revolution that the full practice of freedom in Christ would have brought. Whether he was led by the Holy Spirit in proceeding in this way, let me say as Paul would have said, "I know not!"

As women experienced the saving and liberating power of Christ, they undoubtedly began doing things in their sanctuaries of worship that other women in the society were not free to do. No other religion or philosophy was teaching that there was no difference between male and female. As women who had been suppressed became Christians and were liberated by the Spirit of God, some of them began speaking out in the worship services. This would have been shocking because women were not permitted to speak in public in most cities at that time.

Paul, apparently, had a hard time with the changes that the gospel brought, and he showed indecision and ambivalence about them. He was hard on women in some churches and complimentary of them in others. He even seemed to argue with himself in 1 Corinthians 11.

First, he went back to his Jewish roots and proclaimed the "obvious" superiority of the male because woman originated from

man: "woman was created for the man's sake." Then he remembered
that, in Christ, they were one and the same.

Next, he had a "breakthrough" moment in which he philosophized
that, yes, woman did originate from man, but did not man originate
from woman? And then he surmised, everything originates from God.
It was almost like he was saying, "Why worry about which came first,
the chicken or the egg. God made them both." Then he made a great
statement to the Corinthian church, "Judge for yourself."

In sharp contrast to Paul's harsh words for the women in some of
the churches, he was very complimentary of the women in leadership
positions in the church of Philippi, in Macedonia. The society in
Macedonia was apparently somewhat different than the rest of the
Roman world. There were women in Macedonia who were educated
and property owners.

In Macedonia Paul met with Lydia and helped her in teaching the
gospel. When he wrote to the Philippians, he talked about Euodia and
Syntyche, two women who, he said, had toiled with him in the gospel.
There was no talk in his letter to the Philippians about women keeping
quiet or not teaching men.

So, the question regarding Paul's writings about women is this: Was
God using Paul to command a subservient role for women in the church
until the Second Coming? Or, instead, was Paul struggling with God's
model of equality in a very unequal world as he tried to nurture the
infant church in a hostile environment? I am pretty sure that the
answer is behind door number two.

During his entire ministry, Paul fought against strict adherence to
any laws other than the law of love. I think that he would be aghast if
he knew how Baptists have taken his writings about women and made
some very "unloving" Baptist laws out of them.

In most of the churches where Paul ministered, the women were,
undoubtedly, illiterate and totally inexperienced in public discussion
and debate. Everything in Paul's Jewish background and his experiences in most of the Roman world told him that women were, indeed,
the inferior gender. God really stretched Paul by giving him the assignment of declaring his model of gender equality to the world. It appears
that, in Macedonia, Paul may have gotten a glimpse of what God was
talking about.

We may be like Paul and want our churches to "gradual into" God's
model of equality. We may be a lot like Paul, but let's be realistic. If

equality has not happened after nearly two thousand years, we are not "gradualing" very well.

Some Baptists, I am glad to say, have adopted God's model as their own. Some Baptist denominations ordain women for Christian service and welcome them into leadership roles of pastors and deacons. Other Baptist churches, exercising their rights as congregational bodies, also ordain women for Christian service. But one of the big problems is that those who do often have to suffer the wrath of those who don't.

I knew one very faithful Baptist woman who felt called of God but chose not to be ordained because she knew that her husband would lose his denominational job if she were ordained. She followed her calling by working, unordained, in another denomination. And I knew another devout, lifetime Baptist woman who, after getting a masters degree at the Southern Baptist Theological Seminary, went looking for pastoral opportunities in the Episcopal Church because there was no room for her in the Southern Baptist inn.

Some Baptist missionary agencies are denying young couples the opportunity to live out their calling as missionaries if the wife has ever been ordained. This is worse than Paul telling women to keep their mouths shut and their hair out of sight. How can this happen? This kind of irrational, unscriptural behavior completely baffles me.

When I was in college, I rented a room in the home of Ethel Huber, who was the pastor of the Assembly of God Church in Morgantown. Often, late at night when I was studying, I would hear the unmistakable sound of a woman earnestly praying. I knew that sound because I had been "raised on it," hearing my mother similarly praying hundreds and hundreds of times. Sometimes, Mrs. Huber's voice was so distinct that I could hear my name being called out in her prayers.

I attended an occasional service at Mrs. Huber's store-front church and enjoyed her sermons and the humble people in her congregation. I particularly remember her sermon about the great image of Nebuchadnezzar's dream, foretelling the great kingdoms of the world. This was the first time that I had heard a sermon on that subject, and it still stands out in my mind as my model for that text.

Mrs. Huber was about the business of getting people saved and, by my standards, she was being successful. People were coming to Christ and the church was growing.

I do not believe that the people who were led to the Lord by this woman will be denied access to the Kingdom of God, nor will they be relegated to second-class heavenly citizenship. Nor do I believe that God has withheld any blessings from the Morgantown Assembly of God Church for the past thirty years because they once had a woman pastor.

Most Baptist groups are like other religious groups that cling to a "men-only" mentality. We have been paternalistic for so long that our paternalism breeds more paternalism. We are often critical of the Roman Catholic Church and its policies regarding women and family. We say, "What do they know about women and families? All their decisions are made by a bunch of old men who have never even been married." We are similarly critical of some of the positions of the Mormons who are led by a male president and council of men only.

If we are going to be critical of the Catholics or the Mormons or any other group, we need to take a look first at ourselves and the people whom we are empowering to make the decisions in our Baptist denomination, or our association, or our local church. In a vast majority of cases, these decision makers are men. As I said before, this situation, like a lot of our sins, is self-perpetuating.

It does not look like we are going to "gradual" ourselves out of this. Does this mean that God will have to intervene as he has often done in times past when his people were being held in bondage? I hope not. I hope that we are not as stubborn as Pharaoh when it comes to heeding the call of God to liberate his people. Surely, we can study his Word and accept his plan for the equality of all people in Christ and change our attitudes and practice.

Just think of the energy that we would generate if we removed the bonds from the Baptist women of the world. Think of the impact on a lost and dying world if Baptist women were free to use their full intellects and all of their talents in the ways that God is calling them to minister to others.

We often wonder why Baptists seem to sputter and stall so much. Maybe it is because God has given us an eight-cylinder car to drive for him, and we insist on firing up only half of the cylinders. Maybe he wants us to fire up all eight. It would not kill us to do it. Methodists do it. Episcopalians do it. Pentecostals do it. Lutherans do it. Presbyterians do it. Even some Baptists do it.

Let's do it! Let's humble ourselves, pray, and seek his face, repent of our sin of sexism, and let his women go, so that he can forgive us and use us as examples of his model of equality for the world.

5   . . . Would Call No Man Father

IN MATTHEW 23:9, JESUS SAYS, "DO NOT CALL ANYONE ON earth 'father,' for you have one Father, and he is in heaven." My understanding of this passage is that God is our spiritual Father and that he has given us the responsibility of never placing anyone on earth in that position. This is central to the great Baptist doctrine of the priesthood of the believer. And it assures me that I do not need anyone between me and God because I have a personal Father-son relationship, and that is the way God wants it.

Since Jesus was so clear about this subject, how is it that we get ourselves in such awful predicaments by ignoring his admonition and placing mere mortals between us and our Heavenly Father? Whom do we let get between us and God? Ninety-nine percent of the time, it is a preacher.

During my childhood, I was absolutely in awe of preachers. Being raised in the country, our family was part of a small church which, in fat times, had preaching two Sundays a month and, in lean times, one Sunday a month. The pastors usually lived outside our community, and they often stayed in our home on the Saturday night before "preaching Sunday."

During revival time each year, we would usually be the host family for the evangelist for two weeks. I still have fond memories of the stories that those preachers would tell, and I can still almost hear Dad and one of them downstairs, after I had gone to bed, discussing the deep mysteries of the faith. One of the ways that I came to measure a preacher was by how spectacular or miraculous his conversion and call to the ministry were. The grand champion, as far as I was concerned, was not even a Baptist but a Methodist preacher named Willie Wills. He had grown up in the same community as my mother, and she substantiated his testimony that he was the meanest, fightingest, drinkingest person in the county.

Willie Wills' conversion and call to the ministry happened at the same time, while he was near death, in a coma. According to his testimony, he had a vision while he was unconscious, and he saw himself in a casket floating down New River. He said that he promised God that if he would spare his life, he would live for him. And, boy-oh-boy, did he!

My Methodist preacher grandfather, George Washington Meador, died before I was born, but I always figured that Willie Wills, who had grown up around my grandfather, probably patterned his preaching after my grandfather's example. When Willie preached, he cried, he sweated, he pounded, he whistled through his false teeth, he roared. He preached so hard that he would have to "suck wind" just to keep his tempo going.

Was he effective? I never saw his equal. He could fill the altar at the end of a service like no one else. Being raised in the more staid Baptist church, the sight and sounds of people kneeling at the altar rail, weeping and praying, and then erupting into triumphant shouting, were powerful evidence to me that Brother Willie was, indeed, called of God.

Earl Ward was our pastor when I was ages four to seven, or thereabouts. Brother Ward was a big man, weighing about three hundred pounds. His testimony was that God had rescued him from a life of drinking and fighting. I could easily picture that giant of a man clearing out a beer joint.

He said that when God called him to preach, he tried to argue with and run away from God. When God did finally get hold of him and would not let him go, Brother Ward finally entered the ministry to the great surprise of his old drinking buddies.

These are just two vivid memories out of literally dozens that I recall. I believed preachers every time they said that God had spoken to them, given them a message, or was leading them in some specific endeavor. I rejoiced when they recounted the great evangelistic successes they had experienced in other locations, even when the stories did not square with the success rate they were having at our location. Surely, God was a God of miracles and, just because they were not happening in our church did not diminish their reality. There was probably just something wrong with us.

Then, when I was about twelve years old, I came face to face with an irreconcilable conflict between two of my preacher heroes. Since our little church in the country did not have Sunday night services, my parents and I would often go into the nearby town of Alderson and attend Sunday night services at the historic Old Greenbrier Baptist Church.

Pastor Randolph Johnson was a worthy hero. He was highly educated, at Union Theological Seminary, I think, and an accomplished singer and speaker. He had a deep, cultivated voice that was as rich and full as that of the Great Gildersleeve, a prominent radio personality at the time. I guess that I should compare him to George Beverly Shea for the younger readers. I remember hearing old-timer Homer Ballengee tell Randolph Johnson that he was a greater speaker than the old golden-tongued orator, himself, William Jennings Bryan.

My second hero, Ben Jennings—who, coincidentally, had a son named William Bryan Jennings—entered my world when he came to preach a revival at our little church. He was absolutely the best preacher whom I had ever heard. And, I might add, he is still the best preacher whom I have ever heard.

Everyone in our community was captivated by him, and by the end of that two-week revival, people were standing in the aisles just to hear him preach. People went forward to receive Christ or to rededicate their lives in record numbers. At last, we had a miracle revival in our church.

The baptismal service, conducted Sunday afternoon at the conclusion of the revival, was the greatest such event that most of us had ever experienced. Over a hundred people crowded on the creek bank to see more than thirty people of all ages get baptized.

Our church invited Brother Jennings back the next year for another revival. He came and we had another great two weeks. There was one small difference this year, though. Earlier that year, Brother Jennings had led the church of which he was pastor to withdraw from the fellowship of the Raleigh Baptist Association and, thus, the American Baptist Convention. His sermons were now sprinkled with criticisms and condemnations of the denomination and its seminaries, programs, and leaders. I had no trouble with that. If Brother Jennings expressed such criticisms, then they had to be true.

The next year, Jennings declined our church's invitation to preach another revival. Instead, he solicited our help in conducting a tent revival in Alderson. We helped him set up the tent, passed out flyers, had him stay at our house, and showed up for every night of the revival.

One night, in the middle of his sermon, Brother Jennings asked, "Where is Randolph Johnson?" Good question, I thought. What better opportunity for my two preacher heroes to get together and further the cause of Christ than during this tent revival almost in sight of the Old Greenbrier Baptist Church?

Evidently, word of this got to Randolph Johnson, for my two heroes had a private face-to-face meeting the next day, and they apparently discussed their respective philosophies regarding revivals, denominational integrity, and the role of the pastor in a Baptist church.

That night, Brother Jennings preached on the role of the pastor. He made his case for the strong leader type, called of God to "drive the wagon." He said that he had talked recently with a "prominent Baptist pastor" who said that his role is not to be the leader, but rather to be the servant of the congregation.

"That pastor," Brother Jennings stated strongly, "is not driving the wagon. He is riding on the coupling pole." The coupling pole, for the information of those who never lived on a farm that used horse-drawn wagons, is an extension of the main "backbone" of the frame under the wagon bed. The coupling pole is a sturdy timber that extends behind the wagon bed for about three feet just like a tail. This was a favorite place for kids to ride when the wagon was full of corn, hay, or other cargo.

The metaphor was not lost on the crowd. As they were departing the tent, I heard two members of the Greenbrier Baptist Church talking. One said, "He's right! Randolph Johnson is riding the coupling pole instead of driving the wagon." The other nodded in agreement. This was perplexing to me. How could the two preachers who I was most sure had direct lines to God and who were God-directed be in conflict with each other?

Soon there was a lot of that type of conflict going around. Bob Jones University was turning out a new crop of preachers every year, and they just seemed to swarm north and cover the countryside. And, boy, could they preach.

They were in demand for revivals in many of our small country Baptist churches, but by the time they had left, there was often more dissension than unity in the community. Their sermons rang out with "apostasy," "denial of the Virgin Birth," "denial of the Bible as the infallible Word of God," and numerous other sins that, they seemed certain, had overtaken mainstream Baptists. "The Methodists have gone to the dogs, and the American Baptists and Southern Baptists are right behind them," I heard, about 1950.

The end result of most revivals, then, was that the church either chose to "defellowship" itself from its Baptist association, or there was a split among the members. Often an unaffiliated concrete-block church sprang up in sight of the old affiliated white-steepled church in a community where there were barely enough resources to support one church. In all cases, some people became disillusioned and decided either to become Methodists or to give up on churches altogether.

Then something else happened that forced me to question my complete faith in preachers. The most popular local radio evangelist, Harry R. Peyton, announced that God wanted him to run for congress. That was the most exciting thing that I could imagine.

First, I surmised, God would make him a congressman, then a senator, and then, if God wanted it to happen, Brother Harry would be president. Wouldn't it be wonderful to have political leaders who got their instructions directly from God? God's men in politics, what a great idea! I never considered that Brother Harry might lose. How could he? God had told him to run! He had it made!

I was very surprised and more than a little alarmed when I discovered that my dad was not going to vote for Brother Harry. I considered my dad as being close to the Lord, not as close as the preachers whom God directly talked to, of course, but I was afraid that Dad's decision to vote for someone else meant that he would be voting against God's will. I shuddered to think what might happen to him.

Brother Harry finished last in a big field in the primary election. I pondered for a long time as to why God would tell his man to run for congress and then let him be humiliated in the election—especially after he had told his man that, if he would run, he would win.

By this time, I was totally confused. It seemed as if God was giving contradictory instructions to his preachers—preachers who confidently declared that they were "God's men," were engaged in warfare with other preachers who were just as confident in their position. And then, to top it off, God just hung poor old Brother Harry out to dry!

Then I was rescued by Brother Mustoe, a little fiery banty rooster of a preacher who conducted a successful revival in our church. Sometime during the following year, our church was looking for a pastor and contacted Brother Mustoe. He happened to have two Sundays a month available, so our church called him.

Brother Mustoe had preached fourteen powerful sermons during the revival. His first few sermons as pastor were outstanding, too. Then, the quality of the sermons began to drop off. It seemed that the Lord was not doing his job of giving the preacher the sermons that he wanted preached.

"Brother Dodd," the pastor said to my dad one Sunday morning, "would you lead us in another song? The Lord hasn't given me the message that he wants me to preach yet." I could hardly wait for the song to be over. This was going to be the best sermon ever! It was going to be direct from God without notes or anything. Boy, was I disappointed! God delivered the most rambling, disjointed, uninspiring sermon through Brother Mustoe that I had ever heard.

Guess what? That was not the last time that God neglected to give the pastor the sermon prior to the service. As a matter of fact, God's negligence became the rule rather than the exception.

Thus, Brother Mustoe forced me to do some thinking and realize that there was more than one possibility as to what was happening. Maybe, just maybe, the preacher was messing up and telling us that it was God's fault instead of admitting that it was his. What if it wasn't God who was lazy? What if it was the preacher? What if the preacher was putting himself in a no-risk situation by saying, "God told me to do it," when God had not told him after all?

That was when the light bulb went on. It can't be God. It must be the preacher! I consider myself fortunate to have figured this out at an early age. A lot of Baptists have not figured it out yet, including the poor people who keep sending their hard-earned money to support the lavish lifestyles of media evangelists who claim that God talks to them.

Over the years, I have developed a fairly simple system of evaluating preachers. The ones whom I immediately run away from are the ones who want to place themselves between me and my Heavenly Father. These preachers possess some telling traits. Four examples follow:

Preachers who use "holyspeak"—These preachers have their own language which is designed to assure us that God is in their every thought and action. The first thing we have to do if we are stuck with one of them is to learn to decode their language. For example, when a preacher says, "God wants me to be in congress," the decoded message is, "I want to be in congress. Oh, Lord, please let me be in congress." Or if the statement is, "God hasn't given me the message yet," the decoded message is, "This service is not very important so I did not take the time to prepare for it."

There are thousands more examples. It seems as though some preachers get so caught up in holyspeak that they cannot talk in any other way. It becomes second nature for them to seek to validate everything they say by uttering, "God says," before every statement in much the same way a game leader would validate every action by saying, "Simon says."

Holyspeak can be very intimidating. I knew a man who, after his conversion, became very, very religious. He became the world's best at holyspeak. He never spoke without attributing his ideas and utterances to the Lord.

We had a neighbor named Frank who had a nice two-ton truck, just the vehicle that our religious neighbor wanted. So he went to Frank's house and told him that he wanted to buy the truck. "No," Frank told him, "I don't want to sell my truck. I need my truck." "I am going to go behind your barn and talk to the Lord about this," the religious neighbor said in his best holyspeak. When he returned from his very loud conversation with God, which Frank could plainly hear, he announced that "the Lord told me to buy that truck from you for five hundred dollars." Frank sold him the truck for less than half its value.

Preachers who say that they have a direct line to God—Watch these preachers especially closely. God does not talk to preachers any more than he talks to you. If they will lie to you about this, they might lie to you about anything. These preachers are always experts at holyspeak. They say things like, "The Lord spoke to me, and I heard him just as clearly as you are hearing me now." Or, "God has shown me that it is his will for. . . ."

At this point, you can add almost anything, like, "Brother Blank to be selected as a deacon," or, "this church to revise its constitution and by-laws," or "this church to pay its pastor the average of the male wage earner members of the church," or "this church to enter into a building program." I have heard all of these and many more, and I am sure you have, too. Such preacher sayings are plentiful among Baptists.

All of this is the highest form—or is it the lowest form?—of dishonesty. These preachers are willing to invoke God's name just in order to advance their own ideas. I have seen deacon boards stacked with people who will rubber stamp the every wish of a dictatorial pastor, constitutions and by-laws changed to give dictatorial powers to the pastor, elaborate building plans adopted, and massive debt incurred, all because of the assurance of a pastor that the actions are God's will, as revealed directly to him. Is this not using God's name in vain?

Have you ever noticed what happens when the plans that were attributed to God go awry and the church gets into trouble? That's right. God speaks to the preacher again. "God has told me that my work here is finished," we hear, "and after much prayer, he has shown me that he wants me to resign my position here and move to a new field that he has prepared for me."

Now, if we would just decode what the preacher was saying, maybe we could stop the cycle of calling preachers who try to place themselves between us and our Heavenly Father. What he just said was, "Things have gotten out of hand. I'm going to blow this joint. Anywhere else would be better than here." But what do we do? We believe him and then go out and call someone else who does it to us again.

Preachers who will not let you use their first name—This might seem trivial, but I have observed that this is often the first step toward the dreaded "elevated clergy," which is really the theme of this chapter.

C. I. Scofield, in his reference Bible, came up with a lot of interesting interpretations of the Scriptures. The one that I happen to like the best is one of his most criticized interpretations, the one regarding the sin of the Nicolaitans, referred to in Revelation 2. Scofield believed that the sin of the Nicolaitans was the elevation of the clergy to a level above the rest of the members of the church.

As a Baptist, I am against anything that denies or, in any way, takes away from the equality that we are given in Christ. If Scofield was correct about the Nicolaitans, that puts me in good company because Jesus said, through John, the author of Revelation, that he "hates the deeds of the Nicolaitans."

Names are great equalizers. It makes sense, then, that people who want to be "more equal than the rest of us" would look for some other form of address. Baptists would never use the term "father," because Jesus said not to. But we do use other terms of the preacher's choosing. "The Right Reverend Doctor Uppington" still sounds pretty good to some. The more familiar "Pastor Bill," or "Pastor Smith," is the preference of others. There are numerous other choices.

As you know by now, I am not offended by the term brother or sister when used to refer to a preacher. That is, I am not offended if the term is used in return. When used by both the clergy and laity to refer to each other, it is an equalizer, but if it is only used to refer to the preacher, at the insistence of the preacher, even the term "brother" becomes an "unequalizer."

When I was in my late twenties, I was doing some maintenance work at our church along with the pastor, who was about my age, and another man about ten or fifteen years older than we were. There, in the isolation of three men in a church on Saturday afternoon, the older man called me "Paul" and the pastor "Bob." The pastor let the first "Bob" go unchallenged, but when the second was uttered, he took the time to lecture the older man about the impropriety of talking to "God's man" in a disrespectful manner. "If a pastor lets people call him by his first name, they will not respect him," the pastor said. "It is important that the position of pastor be protected."

Years later, in another Baptist church, I heard a pastor use similar logic to explain why it would be inappropriate for him to participate in a clean-up day at the church. "If the people see me doing things like that," he said, "they will have less respect for me as their pastor."

Preachers who think that their call is superior to yours—A call from God does not have to be miraculous or spectacular, as I thought when I was a little boy, nor is it reserved for the elite few. Everyone who knows Jesus as Savior is called of God.

A call could come in a blinding light like the Apostle Paul experienced or in a vision like Willie Wills had, but there are precious few of those. The call of God to the rest of us is simply seeing something that needs to be done and recognizing that God has equipped us to do it, and that includes preachers. They are saved and called in exactly the same way as the rest of us. They are no more likely to see lights and hear voices than you are.

When I hear the terms "God's man" or "God's anointed," I shudder. These terms are usually used in a sentence such as, "Do not criticize or stand in the way of 'God's anointed' one." This is holyspeak for "Watch out. I am going to take advantage of my position."

I have had a very unpleasant personal experience with this kind of situation. No sooner was I elected chairman of the deacons in a Baptist church than I began to be barraged by members who were accusing the pastor of various dishonest activities.

I quickly confronted the pastor privately about the accusations, and, after a couple of very difficult meetings involving hours of denials, rationalizations, and bluffing, he finally acknowledged that he, indeed, had been dishonest and that he was sorry. We cried, prayed, and embraced, and he promised to make a clean break with it at the next deacons' meeting.

I opened the next deacons' meeting with prayer and then, displaying my most pious face and forgiving manner, I turned the meeting over to the pastor, presuming that he would tell the truth. He immediately started with the premise that the devil was using someone in a high position in our church to undercut his ministry. "That's funny," I thought, "we didn't discuss that in our private meetings. I wonder who is out to get him?"

Before I knew what was happening, all faces turned toward me; it was not the pastor talking, but two of my fellow deacons who were lambasting me with everything they had in their spiritual arsenal. The main theme was that I had no right to disagree with, or criticize, the pastor. He was "God's man," called and set aside for the ministry, and I had better keep my hands off him.

That preacher had played me for the fool. He had pretended repentance, promised to make things right, but had, instead, gone to the two least informed members of the board and got them loaded for bear, or at least for Dodd.

There was nothing I could say or do to reverse the situation. When I reminded the pastor of the things that he had said in our private meetings and the promises that he had made, he denied them all. That was when he put on his most pious face and watched me die.

Soon after that debacle, Rose joined me on a three-week business trip. On our way home, she and I agreed that the best thing for us to do was to go to another church rather than continue to struggle with an impossible situation.

As soon as we got home, I called the pastor, told him of our decision, and asked if we should write a letter to the church, informing the members of our actions. "Brother Paul," he said, "I think you are doing the right thing. I don't want you to put anything into writing; just let me notify the church of your decision. I'll handle it for you, Brother. God bless you." And, of course, he handled it. Not only did he not notify the church, when people asked him, "Where are the Dodds," he told them, "I don't know. I haven't seen them."

As children of God, we are the called of God, each and every one of us, not just our preachers. We are all called to be saints of God. Not just the preachers. We are reminded throughout the New Testament that we are all parts of the same body, blocks in the same building, workers in the same vineyard. We each have our unique talents and "callings," but we are clearly informed that none of us is to think of his or her position in the body as superior or inferior to any other.

Lest you miss my point: preachers are called of God, anointed, sanctified, or any other word you choose to use, in exactly the same way you and I are called, anointed, sanctified, etc. The fact that the preacher is called to different service than you or I, or has been given different gifts than we have been given, does not make that person spiritually superior to you or me in any way.

Baptist, if you are a child of God, there is nothing or nobody superior to you. Jesus wanted us to live by this principle. That is why he told us not to call anyone on earth "father."

We must recognize that God is our Father and that he is jealous of that relationship. In 1 John 3:1, we are instructed to see "how great is the love the Father has lavished on us, that we should be called children of God."

If we are truly the recipients of this great love and the unspeakable privilege of being children of God, why in the world would we then choose to adopt someone like you or me—an earth-bound, mistake-prone fellow-laborer—to be our spiritual father simply because that person happens to be a preacher?

Making us his children cost God everything. It cost him the sacrificial death of his only begotten Son. He is not going to be at all happy if we choose to adopt an earthly spiritual advisor as our spiritual father and try to relegate God to the role of Holy Grandfather.

I am a father and a grandfather. I love my children and my grandchildren. The main difference between the relationship between parent and child and grandparent and grandchild is constancy. When I spend time with my grandchildren, it is a visit. Their parents are the ones who help them make the important decisions, give them constant guidance, and meet their needs. That is what God wants in his relationship with us. He does not want to visit with us occasionally and then leave us in the constant care of a human baby-sitter.

Jesus was careful not to put even himself between us and God the Father, choosing to describe himself as our brother instead of our father. If God did not give the position of fatherhood to Jesus, then I do not believe that he gave it to Peter, or Paul, or any priest, or any Baptist preacher.

We are told in Galatians 4 that people were in need of guardians and tutors only until the coming of Christ. Since his coming, we have the unbelievable privilege of becoming God's children, not his grand-children, nor his second-class children in need of an earthly spiritual father.

I believe that the medieval Catholic Church made a great mistake by forbidding free access to the Bible to its members, relying instead on the study and interpretations of its priests and scholars. Similarly, I believe that we present-day Baptists are making a mistake when we "brainwash" our seminary students rather than educate them. Many young Baptist pastors are not able to lead a congregation in true Bible study because they have only been prepared to dictate doctrine in a dogmatic way.

That same mentality has caused much of our Sunday School literature to provide simplistic, narrow, one-conclusion interpretations of Scripture rather than honest, open, background information which promotes and enhances serious Bible study.

It really upsets me when I read that my denominational leader has announced who God and I want to serve on the Supreme Court, or has decided which political candidate God and I are supposed to support. It also upsets me when Baptist colleges and seminaries tell their preachers-in-training that "God will not hold the deacons responsible for the congregation that you pastor. He will hold you, the under-shepherd, responsible. Therefore, one of your first tasks as a pastor will be to get your deacons under control."

I have come to believe that the splits that I saw in Baptist churches as a kid were not over apostasy, the Virgin Birth, and the Bible as much as they were over the "position of the preacher in the wagon." I simi-larly believe that much of today's denominational warfare is not over doctrinal issues, either; rather, it represents a power move by preachers who believe that they are the only ones who can "drive the wagon" and that, by doing so, they are carrying out God's will. Dictatorial leadership, whether in the church or in the denomination, violates two of the most important traditions of Baptists: democratic, congregational rule and the priesthood of the believer.

My brother-in-law, Elmer, and I swapped notes a few years ago when both of our churches called new pastors. I will relate Elmer's story first. Elmer was initially very impressed by his new pastor. According to Elmer, "That man can really preach the Word." One of the first things that the pastor wanted to work on was the constitution and by-laws of the church. He personally rewrote them and presented them to the church, which adopted them.

Then things started going downhill. There was considerable controversy in the church; every time any disagreement arose about anything, guess who got to make the decision? Was it the congregation? No! The deacons? No! Then, who was it? That's right, the pastor. The new constitution and by-laws said so. People who disagreed with the pastor's decisions were stuck with the option of living with the situation or leaving.

The actions of the pastor became more and more questionable. Eventually, he moved a mobile home onto the church lot for him and his wife to live in. When Elmer and the rest of the deacons confronted him about this, he encouraged them to leave the church if they could not accept his leadership. Some left. Elmer stayed.

Then one Sunday morning, Elmer arrived at the church to find that two Sunday School rooms in the church had been converted into bedrooms for the pastor's children who had moved back home. When Elmer and another deacon confronted the pastor about this, well, you know the story. He encouraged them to leave the church if they could not accept his leadership. Elmer left.

My experience started out similarly but had a different ending. I was also very impressed by our new pastor. Knowing his background and his strong commitment to congregational rule, I was surprised when he stated in his second business meeting that he had studied our church's constitution and by-laws and recommended that we revise them.

When I told this to Elmer, he nodded his head knowingly. But when I told him "the rest of the story," the nodding stopped and his mouth dropped open. "He thought that our constitution and by-laws gave too much power to the pastor," I told him, "and he wanted us to turn that power back over to the congregation."

Elmer is now back in his church because the old pastor had to go when there was no one left in his congregation to pay his utility bill.

They have a new pastor, and the church is slowly healing and growing.

I was elected to the position of moderator in our church. That was one of the tasks that we decided should be handled by a member rather than by the pastor. How is this working? At business meetings, the pastor is just one of the members of the congregation, free to make motions, argue his point of view, and vote his conscience. Some of his motions are approved, some defeated, and he seems perfectly content with that. And, never yet has he told us that God has told him what the church should do.

Why do we accept the fatherhood of dictatorial Baptist preachers? Probably the main reason is that it is easy. We do not have to think, search, or struggle. Why should we? God's man has all the answers for us. Authority is reassuring to many of us. It removes the doubt that we may have in our own judgment. It is easy for us to go to our human spiritual father who will give us God's answer.

Baptists, we are disobeying God when we abdicate our responsibilities as believer-priests and accept an earthly spiritual father. The result of our abdication of our responsibilities is that we have let our Baptist churches and our denominational institutions come under the control of the power seekers. We have been too lazy and unconcerned to carry out one of Jesus' most important admonitions. Our sin of neglect may be greater than their sin of control.

We call a pastor and then permit, or even expect, that person to do the preaching, teaching, Bible study, visitation, evangelism, and ministry for us. If one person is not enough to do it for us, we call a staff. We send the pastor and staff to represent us at local and national conventions.

Then, suddenly, we are awakened by the undemocratic nature of events in our church or denomination, and we wonder how things got out of control. If they are out of control, and they are, it is because we were asleep at the switch.

Jesus warned us. The privilege of being a priest carries with it a great responsibility. As Baptists, we have been enthusiastic about our priestly privilege, but we have not been diligent about carrying out our priestly responsibilities.

When we abdicate our responsibilities, we are not doing the power-seeking preachers any favors either. Some of them end up out of the ministry, disillusioned and wondering "what happened." Others have "revolving-door" churches which attract about the same number of new members as there are older members who are leaving. The most talented ones build large congregations of members willing to let someone else think for them but have trouble keeping members who want to think for themselves.

An old saying that I believe is relevant in our churches and denominations today states that: "Power corrupts; absolute power corrupts absolutely." We know from our observation of world governments and events that power, when it goes unchallenged, does become corrupt. Not sometimes, or once in awhile, but always!

The exact same thing has happened in many Baptist churches, and the fact the power seekers have wrapped it in holyspeak does not change the outcome. Jesus knew that preachers could not handle power any better than kings, or politicians, or any of the rest of us. He knew what he was doing when he instructed us to not place them over us in an elevated spiritual position.

Our Father-child relationship with God is too precious to give up. Rather than the stern deity of the Old Testament, Jesus introduced us to the One whom he called "Abba," or "Papa," or "Daddy." He instructed us to approach the Heavenly Father in the same loving, personal way.

Now, is not God's way far superior to our way of setting up human spiritual fathers who can never, never, never replace our Heavenly Father? What must we do? We must humble ourselves before our Heavenly "Abba," remove any human relationships that stand between us and our relationship with him, reject those who try to be our spiritual superiors, and call no man father.

6   . . . Would Catch Up to the Bible

I AM A RECOVERING FUNDAMENTALIST. I WILL PROBABLY always be in a state of recovery. It is very hard to overcome fundamentalism once you have experienced it, because the temptations to return to it are so great.

The road is easy. You do not have to worry or think. Everything has been taken care of for you. There is a simple answer to everything. The answer is in the Bible, and your pastor knows where to find it. There is only one interpretation of Scripture, and your pastor has it. The rules are clear and unchanging, as long as you do not change pastors or churches.

You hear the same familiar sermon over and over, and once you have accepted Christ, it is never directed at you. Every sermon is some variation on the plan of salvation, so, in your mind, you can direct it toward any unsaved person in the congregation or to the people who should be in attendance.

It makes you feel so good. I love the great emotional highs that I can experience when I listen to a powerful salvation message and join in singing the great salvation hymns like "Jesus Saves" and "Revive Us Again."

If it is all this good, then why have I rejected fundamentalism? Which ones of the fundamentals have I decided are wrong? The answer is none!

I believe as strongly as ever in the divinity of Christ, the Virgin Birth, the bodily resurrection of Jesus, the vicarious atonement of Christ's death on the cross, the inspiration and inerrancy of Scripture,

73

and the literal Second Coming of Christ. I believe that each person is in need of a personal, reconciled relationship with God and that such a relationship is provided by God's grace through Christ. I further believe that this relationship is a free gift which each person must accept, through faith, or reject.

The reason that I am no longer a fundamentalist is not that I disagree with the "fundamentals of the faith," but rather because I disagree with the stifling, legalistic, and backward-looking ways in which these fundamentals are put into practice by many of us who are called Baptists.

Jesus came into the world at a time when the religious life of the society he entered was dominated by conservative theologians called Pharisees. The Pharisees were the fundamentalists of his day, and he could not stand their approach to faith. And they could not stand him or his message, so they plotted to kill him. They wanted their religion to prevent change, not cause it. Instead of using the Scripture to look forward, they were always using it to look backward and to justify their legalism.

If the Pharisees had been successful, there would not be a church today and Christianity would never have happened. Jesus, the radical, understood the Torah and the law better than the Pharisees did. He saw that God's law had a future, not just a past, if it was unselfishly practiced through love, rather than just being selfishly observed.

Paul faced great opposition from a group of conservative theologians in the early church, the people whom we call the Judaizers. Paul could not stand their point of view, and they could not stand his.

The Judaizers believed that Jesus was the Jewish Messiah and demanded that any non-Jew who accepted Christ must accept Judaism also, with all of the accompanying surgery, foods, laws, and rituals. They were determined not to go forward with Christianity, but rather to take Christianity back into a form of Judaism. If the Judaizers had been successful, there would not be a Gentile church today.

Paul, the radical, understood Jesus and his message better than did those in Jerusalem, even some who had walked with Christ. He saw that Jesus' atoning death and offer of the abundant life reached forward and outward to the whole world, not backward and inward to the Jews only.

Martin Luther faced opposition to his doctrine of "justification by faith" from the conservative theologians of his day, the leaders of the

Roman Catholic Church. The church leaders became Luther's avowed enemies, excommunicated him, and then sought to kill him.

They believed that the top-down, ritualized religion that they were dictating to the people was exactly what God wanted. They were afraid to let the people have the Scriptures to read and interpret for themselves. They opposed any use or interpretation of the Scriptures which might encourage individuals to bypass their hierarchy and enter into a direct personal relationship with God through faith.

If Luther's enemies had been successful against him and other radicals with similar convictions, there would be no Protestant churches today. Luther, the radical, understood the plan of salvation better than did the medieval Roman Catholic Church. He recognized the illuminating effect of providing the Scriptures to the people, as opposed to the "dark ages" that were fostered by the policies of sixteenth-century fundamentalists.

John Wesley was opposed by the conservative theologians in the Church of England. Wesley, the radical, had a clearer vision of God's desire for the spreading of the gospel than did the conservative Church of England, and Methodism was born.

Roger Williams could not live in the stifling environment of conservative Puritanism in colonial America, and the Baptist colony of Providence, Rhode Island, was founded. Williams, the radical, started the Baptist movement in America that would become, with Wesley's Methodism, the religion of the country's westward movement. Conservative Puritanism was too backward looking for even God to use to represent himself on the frontier, so he gave the job to us through doors of religious freedom opened by Roger Williams.

Martin Luther King Jr. was opposed by many Baptists in the twentieth century. The opposition to him was overwhelming among white Baptists, and many black Baptists also opposed him because he dared to use the Scriptures to advocate social change rather than just "preaching the gospel."

King, the radical, recognized something that conservative Baptists chose to either deny or ignore: God is a God of justice and equality, and Baptists, as followers of Christ and citizens of the United States, were not living up to either their Christian or constitutional responsibilities.

If we stop for a minute and analyze, we can see that there are many similarities among these fundamentalists from different centuries. Fundamentalists possess three key traits.

The first trait of fundamentalists is that the rules are all set, and one cannot vary from these rules. The rules are all in the Scriptures, and the fundamentalist, alone, knows what God meant; there is no latitude in interpretation. Legalism reigns.

Jesus, while walking through a wheat field one Saturday, pulled off a head of wheat, crushed it into the palm of his hand, blew away the chaff, and ate the grain. The Pharisees had a field day. They charged him with harvesting a crop on the Sabbath, with threshing grain on the Sabbath, with winnowing grain on the Sabbath, and with preparing a meal on the Sabbath.

Sometimes, when studying the letters of Paul, we get the impression that he had to spend more time explaining that circumcision was elective surgery than he did preaching the gospel. He was constantly fighting against those who wanted to force the Gentile Christians to observe Jewish law. He even had to confront Peter and point out his hypocrisy.

Luther, Wesley, Williams, King, and other reformers within the Christian Church through the centuries have had to fight one thing more than any other: an ingrained, status-quo-defending, conservative establishment that was looking backward to their rules and traditions rather than looking forward to living out the Christian gospel.

I like what Paul said in Philippians 3:13: "Brothers, I do not consider myself yet to have taken hold of it. But one thing I do: Forgetting what is behind and straining toward what is ahead. . . ." Paul was so excited about his future as a child of God that he did not have time to focus on the past.

I am certain that he would say the very same thing if he were here today trying to exhort Baptists to catch up to the gospel instead of trying to enforce our own forms of legalism. Baptist legalism varies from group to group, seminary to seminary, church to church, and we all are guilty of it to some extent.

Some of the examples of legalism that I have been exposed to, and expected to fully accept as a member of a particular congregation, include: the King James translation is the only true Bible; creation occurred in six literal days; psychiatry is of the devil; Halloween is of the devil; women cannot teach males beyond their teens; no mixed gender swimming; no alcohol; no fishing on Sunday—or swimming, or golf, or anything else that might be fun; no purchase of food or anything else on Sunday; a pre-tribulation rapture of the true believers; no tobacco; no Sunday School literature; people tainted by divorce cannot hold church office or teach; no dancing; no card playing; no movies; and the list could go on and on.

It may not be wrong to have some of these on a list of beliefs. The problem arises when they are given equal or greater status than the important things of being a Christian and living a fruitful Christian life. A fruitful life is measured by the production of the fruits of the spirit: love, joy, peace, patience, kindness, goodness, faithfulness, gentleness, and self-control. A fruitful life is not measured by how well we follow a list of Baptist legalistic "don'ts."

Jesus had little time for and less patience with the demands of backward-looking religious folk that he adhere to a bunch of nit-picky rules. It seems logical, then, that we should be concerned with living the life that he taught us, rather than being a slave to a bunch of rules just to please a preacher and the people in a congregation.

We moved to Ravenna, in northeastern Ohio, many years ago. When I had first gone there to interview for the job, I had asked one of my future co-workers, "Is there a Baptist church here?" "There are a bunch of Holy Rollers out on Route 5," was the response.

Soon after we joined the church out on Route 5, the pastor and a deacon came calling at our home. The pastor asked if I would teach a Sunday School class that would consist of high school juniors and seniors and the church's two or three college students.

After I agreed to take the class, the pastor told me that there were two things that must be emphasized. I eagerly awaited his instruction. The two great sins of the young people of this Baptist church that must be condemned, I was then told, are going to movies and roller skating. His instruction seemed irrelevant to the great issues of the day.

To put this in better perspective, this was during the 1960s, the time when young people were dealing with the gigantic issues of civil rights, the war in Vietnam, and the whole counterculture movement. The college students in my class were from Kent State University, one of the most explosive campuses in the country, which was located only four miles from the church. Just how out of touch were we if our emphasis at that time and place was getting our Baptist young people to stop going to movies and to stop roller skating?

I still agreed to teach the class. However, I told the pastor that he would have to handle those topics of movies and roller skating, because I probably did not share his perspective on them.

The next church that we moved to was in Caldwell, in southeastern Ohio. We moved next door to our new pastor, a wonderful down-to-earth man named Roy Wikander, and quickly became close friends with him and his family. I was pleased to find that, in our new church, we loved roller skating; but I was to discover that we were not overly fond of dancing.

I also renewed my acquaintance with a great man, Charlie Boyles, when we moved to Caldwell. I had first met Charlie while I was a student at West Virginia University, and one of our agricultural classes had a lab at the animal husbandry farm which Charlie managed. All the members of our class agreed that Charlie was one of the most enthusiastic, energetic, inspirational people whom we had ever met. I also discovered that Charlie and his family were active leaders in their Baptist church in Morgantown.

When we got to Caldwell, I was overjoyed to find that Charlie now worked for Ohio State University as the manager of a research farm in the Caldwell area. I was surprised to find out, though, that the Boyles family were members of the local Methodist church. Charlie taught the adult Bible class, and his wife Virginia was the organist and choir director.

The next time I saw Charlie, I asked him why he had become a Methodist. "The first Sunday after we moved here, we were in the Baptist church," Charlie said, "and we had every intention of joining that church. But you know something," he continued, "some people from the church came to visit us, and it seemed that the only thing we talked about that night was the sin of dancing; and we had pictures of our girls in their ballerina dresses hanging on the wall." Charlie readily agreed with me that he may have jumped to a conclusion too quickly, but his next statement was similar to statements that I have heard many times from hard-charging people like him. "Don't get me wrong," Charlie said, "Roy Wikander is a fine Christian man, and there are a lot of good people in that church, but I am just not going to invest my time in a church that focuses on insignificant things."

As I said before, one thing that we loved in our new church was roller skating. Once a month, our church would rent a rink in Marietta and go roller skating. I was amused by the irony of this activity being church-sponsored and guilt-free, and looked forward to an opportunity to share my amusement with the pastor.

The perfect opportunity presented itself on the night after one of our church outings to the rink while Brother Roy and I were driving together to a meeting on mental retardation in Cambridge. "Didn't we have a great time last night?" he asked. "Do you know that we had over seventy-five people there?"

"You really like skating, don't you Brother Roy?" I asked.

"I love it!" he replied.

"It is great to put your arm around your wife and hold her hand while you go around the floor, keeping time to the music, isn't it?" I continued.

"Yeah, I really love it!" he said. This led to a discussion of my previous pastor's opinion of skating that we disagreed with, but we had to consider the possibility that the only thing that kept us from committing the sin of dancing at the roller rink was that we had wheels on our feet.

We tried to analyze just what it was about dancing that made it a sin and we settled, for a moment, on an old Baptist idea that "dances are where girls get pregnant." But then I remembered that I had grown up in a community which was so Baptist that no one, including me, had ever even learned how to dance. But, somehow, girls still got pregnant. And the frequency of that happening seemed to correlate with an event other than dancing.

That event, I was reluctant to admit, was revival meetings. Young people would walk in out of the hills to the services, take a liking to someone during that two-week period, and walk each other home after the services. As a result, pregnancies happened. Since we were both unwilling to blame revival meetings for pregnancies, we discussed that maybe we should not put the blame on dancing either.

The conversation gradually began to lighten, and Brother Roy eventually smiled at the humor in the situation and confided that he had always figured that he would be a good square dancer, but he did not know if his wife would approve.

A second trait of fundamentalists is that they are always "going back" to something. I am as nostalgic as the next person. I can get completely lost in reminiscences of my life as a child, life on the farm, my beloved parents, events with my brothers and sisters, favorite pets, holidays, rides in the snow, jumping into the old swimming hole, going squirrel hunting, fishing in the Greenbrier River, and other events that stick indelibly in my memory.

I clearly remember the years when Rose and I were dating. We still stir the fires of romance by talking about those wonderful times and the early days of our marriage. She was so beautiful, and those days were just magic. I love recalling the joy generated by the births and accomplishments of our two boys. I remember their first steps, their first words, their first Christmases, their first days of school, their successes and frustrations in little-league sports, and their good report cards. We had the greatest little boys who ever lived.

I have always been a history buff. By the time I was ten years old, I had read every history book in our home and had probably read *Gone with the Wind* three times. My imagination was so vivid that I would try, mentally, to transport myself back in time so I could help Hector and his Trojans repel the Greek army, or be with Alexander the Great on his conquests, or accompany Hannibal crossing the Alps with his elephants, or be the factor that would tip the scales so Lee could, at last, win the Battle of Gettysburg.

I read *Gone with the Wind* in complete ignorance that Clark Gable had played Rhett Butler on the silver screen and was, thus, what everyone else in the world thought Rhett Butler looked like. My image of Rhett Butler looked a lot like me, a few years older and with a moustache.

The past can be wonderful, but it is not the only dimension of time with which we need to be concerned. If I was in love with Rose only as she was at age eighteen, we would not have much of a marriage. If I did not think that she was as beautiful today as she was thirty or forty years ago, we would both be miserable. If I was not as proud of our sons as mature men, husbands, and fathers as I was of their childhood accomplishments, I would be missing the great joys of "mature" parenthood.

Similarly, if my time horizon did not extend beyond the present, I would not have the vision needed to plan for tomorrow and all the other tomorrows that God may give me. The past is important, but it is the past. The present is important, but it is inescapable because it is already here. But the future, ah, the future—that is where the great opportunities lie, and that is the time dimension for which we can plan and in which we can make a difference. That is where our focus should be directed.

Jesus came to bring change to the world. He came to teach and demonstrate that it was God's purpose in the world to bring God and people, and people and people, together in love relationships.

But the religious leaders said, "let's go back to the law"; they contended that what God wanted was the legalistic, elitist, exclusionist, hollow, self-righteous, religious world that they were presiding over. They could not have any compassion for those who were sick, suffering, starving, or in need of God's forgiveness because they were too busy looking back to some nuance of the law and making sure that it was being followed to the letter. They were so busy looking back to Abraham, Moses, and the other patriarchs that they could not recognize the Son of God, even though Moses and the prophets foretold him.

Baptists, we are great at looking back. We seem to always be longing for those great days of our past when fundamentalism allegedly reigned and fundamentalists were allegedly in charge.

Some of us even look as far back as John the Baptist and are convinced that he was the founder of Baptists, and that we have existed, continuously, since then. Others look back at the godly settlers of our country and long for the spiritual atmosphere that must have existed when everyone was close to God. Others look back to the prayerful days of the founding of our country, with George Washington on his knees and the framers of the Constitution spending more time in prayer than in composition. Others look back to the days of the frontier and the move west, when every man had his wife, his axe, his rifle, and his Bible, and set out with God's blessings to kill the Indians and tame the land.

Others look back to the days of the Civil War and see a prayerful Abraham Lincoln weeping for his country, while others see Robert E. Lee and Stonewall Jackson giving their Baptist-like testimonies and holding evangelistic services and prayer meetings for their soldiers before going into battle. (I know some people look back to the latter. I have seen some atrocious, self-serving movies made by Christian colleges which showed it that way.)

There is just a great longing in some of us to go back to that former state of existence when we apparently were a truly fundamentalist, Christian nation. We all know that it is back there somewhere and we must go back to it. Back to basics, back to God, back to the Bible, back to the faith of our fathers is our desire.

When did this perfect state of fundamentalism exist? I have scanned back through my lifetime and have been forced to conclude that it must have been before I was born.

I was born during the Great Depression, and I do remember that people were more helpful to others because everyone was in need. Maybe the time of the Great Depression was a time of great spirituality. No, that can't be. No one wants to go back to the Great Depression.

I remember during World War II that there was a great amount of prayer and church attendance. But we do not want to go back to the horrors of that era. Besides, that could not have been the golden age of fundamentalism. The country was led out of the Depression and through most of World War II by the most liberal president in our nation's history, Franklin Delano Roosevelt, and he was surrounded by a whole bunch of liberal, freethinking, intellectual advisors. Nope. That wasn't it.

I attended a one-room school for eight years during the late 1940s and early 1950s, and I remember that some of the teachers led us in Bible readings and prayer. Nobody objected, but then everyone who lived in our little community was either Baptist or convinced that they should be, so there was no reason to object. Maybe that is what we should go back to.

I do remember one little girl who did not attend our school, though. She was the relative of a family in our community that was raising her, but because her hair was too "naturally curly," she had to be transported more than twenty miles to the nearest segregated school for blacks.

No, I do not believe that we were quite achieving God's standards then. If that was it, I do not want to go back to it.

When, then, was the great period of spirituality in the United States? Could it have been during the Civil War? Surely there was a lot of praying going on then. I have heard that the devout Baptists in the South were certain that the Confederacy would win the Civil War because Jefferson Davis was a praying man.

But then someone wondered about the quandary that God would be in if Abraham Lincoln was a praying man, too. Abraham Lincoln did, indeed, pray. Once, when a preacher asked him if he was praying for God to be on his side, Lincoln told the preacher that instead of trying to get God on his side, he was praying that he was on God's side, for God was always on the side of right.

Lincoln was surrounded by fundamentalist Baptists all of his life. His father and mother became members of the Little Mount Separate Baptist Church in Kentucky about the time of his birth. This church did not agree with the Philadelphia Confession of Faith, used by many Baptists in the United States, and was an early independent, fundamentalist church. When the Lincolns moved to Illinois, Tom Lincoln and his new wife became members of the Pigeon Creek Baptist Church.

But Abe never accepted fundamentalist Baptists, nor did they accept him. Many Baptists of Lincoln's day called him an infidel, an atheist, and a freethinker because of his belief in universal salvation. He was hounded by Baptists all through his political career by the charge that he did not believe in the Virgin Birth and had once said that Jesus was the son of Joseph, not the Son of God.

The religion of the leaders of the Confederacy may have been closer to orthodox Baptist theology, but let's stop and consider what they were engaged in. They were waging a war of rebellion against their legally constituted government and fighting to preserve human slavery. This was also the time when brother was killing brother. This could not possibly be the time we long to go back to.

Let us go back to 1776 and the birth of our nation. Surely this was the time when the hand of God was on our nation's leaders like no other. Therefore, they must have been fundamentalists, right? Wrong!

George Washington was not a Baptist, nor a fundamentalist. He was raised in the Church of England and went through the ritual of membership in that body. But Washington, like Thomas Jefferson and many other of the colonial leaders, was a Deist.

The most concise description that I could give of the Deists of early America would be that they believed in God, but little else. They were skeptical about creeds and sacraments, and they were very philosophically curious.

The "Father of our Country" lived the good life of a wealthy country gentleman. He danced, played cards, made and drank hard liquor, bet on horse races, and, after attending church, did all sorts of things on Sunday. Baptists of Washington's time were as critical of his spiritual life as later Baptists would be of President Lincoln.

Our second President, John Adams, was raised in the fundamentalist, theocratic state of Massachusetts where Puritanism reigned supreme. But by the time Adams made his mark on the national scene, he was a practicing Unitarian.

Probably the greatest contribution that Baptists made in the forming of our country was through the influence of a few Baptist preachers in Virginia who convinced Jefferson and others to include separation of church and state in the Constitution. Ironically, that is the feature of our Constitution that some Baptists today, joining with other fundamentalists, are trying to discredit or repeal.

Was, then, the golden age of fundamentalism the indeterminate period of the settling of the frontier? Probably not.

The percentage of the westward-moving settlers who had made any formal or public commitment to faith was very low. Some did take a Bible with them, but often their religion was a mixture of superstition and some concepts from the Bible. The near absence of religion on the frontier made it fertile ground for the revivals of the Second Great Awakening. And Baptists grew because of those revivals.

The golden age of fundamentalism in America, then, had to be in colonial Massachusetts. Settled by the Pilgrims and the Puritans, the colony of Massachusetts stands as the only example of a fundamentalist government in this country. The government in the colony of Massachusetts was created by the strictly devout colonists. Adult males who were church members were the only ones who were allowed to vote. The laws were based on their interpretation of Scripture. Government leaders were not expected to answer to the people; they were expected to answer only to God. (Sound good? There are some Baptists advocating the same type of government and leaders for our country today.)

The Massachusetts colonists had the death penalty. People could be executed for cursing, hitting their parents, or denying God, whatever that means.

We all know what they did to nineteen elderly people when a group of girls accused them of being witches. They went into a state of hysteria and killed them.

They had stocks and pillories and public floggings for drunkenness, profanity, sexual immorality, kissing your spouse in public, and many, many other offenses. Legalists develop long lists.

Why does this sound familiar? This sounds a lot like some governments in the world today—governments that repress free expression, execute people for minor offenses, cut off people's hands and ears, and demand adherence to a single, narrow-belief system.

What do we call those governments? That's right! Fundamentalist! Certainly not Christian fundamentalist, but isn't the similarity more than a little bit frightening?

The way the fundamentalists ran Massachusetts was the reason that Roger Williams became a Baptist and fled to Rhode Island, and it was the reason that John Adams became a Unitarian. People with minds of their own could not survive in such an environment. Neither can people today. This is a big factor in the back-door exodus of so many Baptists from our churches and denominations, especially our young people.

Rather than the United States being founded solely by colonists wanting to establish a fundamentalist society, the majority of colonists who came to the New World were trying to escape from various forms of Christian fundamentalism being imposed on them in Europe. As we look back at the history of our great country, then, we find only one instance of a fundamentalist Christian government, and the success of that government is in great question.

When we look at the great events, documents, and happenings in our history, we are hard pressed to find one of them which was done by a fundamentalist or which was advocated by any group of fundamentalists. What we do find is that the opposite is often true. The fundamentalists were the ones leading the opposition to needed change. We have seen this in our lifetime as they have fought bitterly against one of the most important legal and moral events in our nation's history, passage of the Civil Rights Act.

The great occurrences of our nation's history were brought about by people who were intellectually open, had questioning minds, and were not bound hand and foot by a lot of unnecessary rules—people like Washington, Adams, Jefferson, Lincoln, and Roosevelt. And people like Franklin, Hamilton, Monroe, Madison, and numerous others. They were all progressive visionaries looking to the future that could be, not conservative reactionaries looking backward to a past that had been or maybe never was.

Similarly, the great events and transitions of Christianity were caused by the radicals—Jesus, Paul, Luther, Wesley, Williams, King, and others—not by reactionaries. But those realities do not stop the fundamentalists. They simply look back at history and revise it all the way back to John the Baptist to the way they think it should be. They shamelessly attribute fundamentalist beliefs and lifestyles to the heroes of the faith and the heroes of our nation.

I cringe when I hear pompous statements like "Saint Augustine was born again" or "we are sure now that Martin Luther was really a Christian" from people who think that they have made a great discovery. I have no more patience for people who sit around figuring out who, in history, meets their criteria to really be a Christian than I do for people who sit around judging who is really a Christian today.

The third characteristic of fundamentalists, and perhaps the saddest, is that love is lost in legalism. The priest, in Jesus' story of the Good Samaritan, refused to assist the man who had been beaten and left beside the road to die. The priest knew that the law said that if he touched a dead man, he would be unclean for seven days. The man might die while he was helping him; then he could not carry out his temple duties. So, because of legalism, he left the man to die.

I have known young Baptist women who were being beaten and otherwise abused by their husbands, even to the extent of their lives being in danger, while their families refused to help them get out of the terrible situation.

Why in the world would a parent of a woman who is living under the threat of death from her husband not do everything in his or her power to rescue the daughter? I have heard some great answers.

"It is God's will for them to stay together." What kind of a God would want a person to remain in a situation where she is being constantly abused? Certainly not the God of love that I serve.

"Divorce is a sin." I do not think divorce is nearly as big a sin as knowing that your daughter is being abused and demanding that she remain in the situation.

"What will people think? I am a deacon." Some will judge you and think that you are a disgrace. Some will think that you are only human and forgive you for doing what they may even think is wrong.

But your daughter will rise up and call you "blessed." And the One who told the story of the Good Samaritan will probably say, "At last! One of those Baptists understood what I was talking about."

It is a great shame that Baptist parents are sometimes as useless as the priest in the story of the Good Samaritan. They are useless because their legalism has blocked even one of the most natural emotions that God created us to possess: protective love for our own children. If, when a person is in his or her time of greatest need, our religion only condemns, does nothing to help the person in trouble, and ties our hands so that we cannot be of help, what good is it?

I once worked across the hall from a young man who told me that he did not attend church but wanted to get started. When I asked him where he lived, I found out that he had just moved into a new home in sight of a Baptist church. I knew the pastor of that church, so I described him in glowing terms and strongly urged the young man to attend. He promised me that he would.

On Monday, I asked him, "How was church?" He said that he had not gone, but was evasive as to why he had not followed through and attended. When I pressed him for a reason, he shared the following account: "We will not be going to that church. One of our neighbors who is a member of that church visited my wife last Friday," he continued, "and she told my wife that she was going to go to hell for smoking cigarettes and wearing shorts."

Now, wouldn't a plate of cookies and a friendly get-acquainted chat have been a better evangelistic approach? Would it not have been better to find out if there was anything that the new, young neighbor needed and meet that need, instead of condemning her?

Jesus told everyone who would listen that something was wrong with a religion that identifies and condemns sin, judges and punishes sinners, and leaves love out. As a matter of fact, he said that if true religion were to be condensed down into one word, that word would be love. Love of God and love of other people, he said, was the sum and substance of God's law. "Since God so loved us, we also ought to love one another" (1 John 4:11). It is not good enough just to love those who love us in return. "Love your enemies and pray for those who persecute you" (Matt. 5:44), he instructed us. Further, "If anyone says, 'I love God,' yet hates his brother, he is a liar" (1 John 4:20).

We should notice that the love that we are commanded to extend to others is never conditional as to whether the other person has sinned, or sinned repeatedly, or treated us unkindly. We are told to love, and we are not given any alternative. If we do not extend love, regardless of the circumstance, we are breaking God's law. We are sinning, big time.

We are engaged in spiritual warfare and love is the only—I repeat—the only weapon that we have in our arsenal. Evidently, some people in the early church got this message and put it into practice. I have heard that some first-century Romans noticed the uniqueness of the early Christians. One person noted that most Romans were so self absorbed that they did not even take adequate care of their own families. The Jews, the person said, took care of their own. But the Christians, he marvelled, try to take care of everyone.

Baptists, the message we have is dynamite! Shame on us for presenting another message! We are charged with presenting the same message that Jesus lived and preached and eventually died for.

This message caused the time of Christ on earth to become the pivotal point in history. The message was so powerful that it could not be quieted by the Pharisees, the Caesars of Rome, or by any other power that has opposed it down through the centuries.

This message has the power to change lives, change families, change countries, and change the world. Remember, the charge against the early Christians was that they were "turning the world upside down." And they did that extremely well.

We need to recognize that we have not gotten out ahead of the message. The message of the Bible is not something we need to "go back to." The message from God in the Bible is light years ahead of us. Our challenge is to catch up to it.

The message is well described in 1 Corinthians 13. There Paul tells us that even if we sound like angels, have the gift of prophecy, have all knowledge, have the faith to move mountains, give all our possessions to the poor, and even give our bodies to be burned in an ultimate sacrifice, and have not love, we are nothing.

Baptists, there is a world out there with fields that are white unto harvest, waiting for us to present and live the message of Christ. Our task is not to be constantly looking back, trying to prevent change, grasping for what we think once existed. Our task is to recognize our indebtedness to Christ for what he did for us and accept the role he has for us—being as much like him as possible in our relationships with others.

The Bible has the answers. If his people who are called Baptists would catch up to the Bible, we would be concerned about "turning the world upside down," not wasting time trying to turn back the clock.

7   . . . Would Consider Their Adjectives

WHILE WORKING FOR THE UNITED STATES DEPARTMENT OF Agriculture, I twice had the privilege of representing our government on scientific missions in Hungary. The first time I was there was in 1985 while the country had a Communist government, and the second time was in 1991, after the collapse of Communism.

In 1985 Peter Szabo, my gracious host and interpreter, quietly arranged for me to attend Sunday morning services at a Baptist church in Budapest. No cameras and no fanfare, but no matter, I was able to worship God in a Baptist church in Budapest. I was excited to find that the pastor was Imre Szakacs (So-cots), a Hungarian Baptist leader who had been described to me by Glenn Igleheart, who had met Szakacs at a meeting of the Baptist World Alliance.

I was very impressed and moved by the services. They began at 9:00 A.M. with an hour of prayer, followed by the 10:00 A.M. worship service. About three hundred attended, and everything was familiar, except the Hungarian language and the tingle in the communion wine. Szakacs was a powerful preacher, moving agilely about the pulpit and up and down the stairs to the auditorium level despite the fact that he had only one leg and used only one crutch.

Peter, a Roman Catholic, found the sermon to be very interesting. "It was the story of the sheep and the shepherd," he told me at the end of the service. "The shepherd was the gate to the sheep pen. I have heard this story before."

When I had been preparing for that first trip to Hungary, whenever I felt any apprehension about going to an "atheistic country behind the

Iron Curtain," I would just hum a few bars of "If Jesus goes with me, I'll go anywhere," and that would take care of it.

Boy! Did my ignorance show. Not only did I get to participate in a wonderful Baptist worship experience; I found God everywhere. There were Christian crosses at virtually every rural-road intersection.

On Saturday, when we went into the beautiful Matthias Church, which was built in the thirteenth century in the historic castle district of Budapest, people were praying even as tourists were shooting pictures. As I stood on top of the hill overlooking the city of Szekszard, I looked down at the old brown church where the great composer Ferenc Liszt had worshipped as a young man and had first presented some of his great works.

I had my picture taken in the shade of a small tree beside the Great Church of Debrecen. Peter translated the story on the marker beside the tree. The marker told of a long, heated debate centuries ago between the Calvinist pastor of the great church and the local Catholic priest about what constituted the "True Church." "If your church is a true church," the priest had stated, in exasperation, as he pulled a small twig from a nearby plant and stuck it into the ground, "then this branch will grow up to be a tree."

I would not be surprised if that Calvinist pastor watered that twig every day of his life. I know that I would have. However, the message to me was that not only was there a great church in Debrecen to bear witness of the presence of God; there was also a very old tree and a marker, to boot, also bearing witness.

On a mountaintop near beautiful Lake Balaton, I went into a church that was first built about the year 1000, and parts of the original structure were still in use. Me take Jesus to Hungary? What kind of a misguided ego trip had I been on? Not only was Jesus already there; I saw evidence that he had been there for at least one thousand years before I got there.

In 1991 I went back to the same Baptist church on my first Sunday there and renewed my acquaintance with Imre Szakacs. This time I had my camera, took pictures inside and outside of the church, and even had my picture taken with Szakacs. He wanted me to send copies of the pictures of him to his relatives in New York. Democracy is wonderful.

The following week, as I was working with scientists of the Research Institute for Soil Science and Agricultural Chemistry, one of the researchers named Geza (Gay-za) told me that his uncle had seen me at church on Sunday. Geza told me about his work in another Baptist church and invited me to visit his church and his family the next Sunday.

The service was wonderful. Once again, an hour of prayer at 9:00 A.M. preceded the worship service. Geza explained that the 9:00 A.M. prayer time on the first day of the week is a tradition among Hungarian Baptists which began many years ago when some Baptist leader wanted to follow Acts 3:1, which describes the ninth hour as "the hour of prayer." He said that although everyone now knows that the ninth hour is really three o'clock, the tradition has stuck.

Geza's wife interpreted the worship service into English for a significant group of worshippers from the United States, western Europe, Africa, and Asia, as we met in a room at the back of the sanctuary. After church, we went to Geza's home for an "American" Sunday dinner of fried chicken, mashed potatoes, slaw, and corn bread, prepared in my honor. There I began to get acquainted with this wonderful family.

The oldest daughter was about eighteen, out of school and hoping to be able to go to a Christian college. She had already been part of an evangelistic missionary effort into Spain. The son, in his mid-teens, was debating about becoming either a banker or a missionary. The little daughter, about six or seven years old, seemed only concerned about charming the funny American visitor.

Geza's mother-in-law, who lived with them, told me proudly that her husband and Geza's father had both been "pietists" who had preached throughout the years of Communism. When I confessed that I did not understand the term "pietist," she explained that this meant that they had refused to compromise their message to conform to the edicts of the government and that, as a result, they had been denied the licenses needed to preach legally.

Later that afternoon, Geza took me to a huge apartment complex nearby where he had started conducting Bible studies. He was so encouraged by the response he was receiving from the residents that he had inquired about the price of some vacant land in the vicinity as a possible church site.

It was impossible to spend time with Geza and not catch sight of some of his vision for his family and his church, and his desire to bring the gospel to his community, his country, and the world. It was obvious that the doors of opportunity were wide open for reaching thousands, even millions of people with the gospel. What Geza and others like him needed was a little bit of help: money to buy a small plot of land for a church, scholarship help for the education of their children who felt led to enter Christian service, and Christian training for the many who were willing to be the "laborers."

When I asked Geza if we Americans were providing any of this needed assistance to the Baptists in Hungary, I got a strange answer. "During the forty years of Communism, all of our Baptist churches worked together in close fellowship and love," he said. "Now, since we no longer have Communism, the Americans have come, and they are causing us to disagree and become divided."

"How can this be?" I asked. "What are they doing to cause dissension?" Geza's reply totally flabbergasted me. "They want our churches to sign papers about what we believe about the tribulation period," he said. "Do you know what that means?" "I sure do," I responded, in disgust and despair. "This means that the premillennialists have gotten here."

"I am so discouraged about what they are doing," Geza said. "Why is this so important? Some churches are signing the papers and others are refusing, so now there is no fellowship between some of our churches. Although I have always been a Baptist, when I get the new church started, I do not think it will be a Baptist church."

Can you blame him? How stupid are we? Can't we see what they need and what they don't need? Here was a man who, along with his family, had struggled against "principalities and powers," often illegally, for forty years to keep the gospel message going forth in a Communist society. Now he could use some help from us Baptists in America, and just a little help would go a long, long way. But, instead of help, what did we give him?

As unbelievable as it seems, instead of asking what was needed, or instead of seeing the obvious needs, we gave him a hundred-year-old, unsolvable, unprovable doctrinal dispute which has absolutely nothing to do with where anyone of us is going to spend eternity or how we live the Christian life. This resulted in strife and bickering instead of furthering the gospel of Christ.

Geza and his fellow Baptists were in the same awkward situation in which Paul and the early Gentile churches found themselves when the well intentioned but ignorant people came from Jerusalem and demanded that all believers be circumcised in order to be true Christians. I am afraid that modern-day "Americanizers" can be just as disruptive and destructive as were the first-century Judaizers.

Think about this: it may be that some of your missionary offerings are being used to promote this type of misguided "modern-day circumcision." What a contrast to the good work of the Gideons, who are providing copies of the Bible and trusting the Holy Spirit, and to others who are working to support the churches there instead of trying to force-feed divisive doctrines.

"Premillennialist" is like a lot of our Baptist adjectives—relatively harmless as a point for discussion but terribly destructive when it becomes dogma and a prerequisite to Christian fellowship. What do you think of when you see the word *premillennialist* on the sign of a Baptist church?

My reaction is that here is a group of people who have made up their minds about something that they know little or nothing about. I know that they have chosen to "take a stand" for a teaching that accomplishes nothing.

I know that they have no difference of opinion about the events of the next coming of Christ. They think they have God in a neat little box, which assures them that there will soon be a rapture of the true believers, followed by a seven-year tribulation period. Then the Lord will come again, conquer the antiChrist, and rule the world for one thousand years. It may happen that way. It may not.

One thought that haunts me any time I am confronted by any "end-of-time" person or group that claims to know exactly what is going to happen when the Lord returns is that when he came the first time, the ones who "knew" exactly what his first coming was going to be were the ones who did not even recognize him when he came. A lot of people, including myself, do not find the Scriptures to be so specific that we can spread a "premillennial calendar of events" all the way across the front of the church and trust it as indisputable fact.

We should not expect the Hungarians to have developed a detailed, Americanized premillennial dogma. You see, they did not have the Scofield Bible, which is the only Bible in which I have been able to find the doctrine of a pre-tribulation rapture.

I remember a Bible study on the subject once in which the pastor told those of us who had older editions of the Scofield Bible that we needed to look at the footnote in our Bibles in order to fully understand

2 Thessalonians 2:3. Scofield was so committed to the concept of a pre-tribulation rapture that he replaced the phrase "falling away" with the wording "taking away" in the footnote of his early Bibles. This meant that the passage now read, "that day shall not come, except there come a taking away first, and that man of sin be revealed." There is that neat little rapture in a box, compliments of Scofield.

I clearly remember the response of the chairman of the deacons to this teaching. "Pastor," he admonished, "right above that footnote is a black line. Below that line it's Dr. Scofield talking, and above that line it's God talking."

My bottom line about the adjective "premillennial" is that it is fun to talk about; it is an interesting speculative teaching; and it may surprise me some day by being accurate. However, to lead with this as a summary of who we are and what we believe does nothing but scare people away and create dissension among believers.

Our message is not how or when the end of time will occur. There are enough other denominations and sects obsessed about that. Let us present the truth of the need for each of us to find God's plan for our lives through a relationship with the crucified, risen, and coming-again Savior, and not waste time fighting about the details of the end of time.

Our much-used adjective "independent" is a redundancy, when coupled with Baptist. What difference is there between a Baptist and an independent Baptist? About the same difference as there is between an Angus cow and a black Angus cow.

As Baptists, we are, by our very nature, independent. We believe that each of us is answerable to God and must enter into a personal saving relationship with God through Christ. We further believe that we, as saints and priests, are entitled to study the Scriptures for ourselves and communicate directly with our Heavenly Father.

We believe that we are free to affiliate ourselves with the congregation of believers which most closely agrees with our experiences and understanding, and to change that affiliation at any time.

The Baptist church with which we choose to affiliate has the same freedom to affiliate with any, or none, of the various groupings or alignments of Baptist churches that exist. Our Baptist church is then free to change affiliations or withdraw from all affiliations, as determined by the will of the congregation.

I have been in many Baptist churches and have never found one that was not independent. Each one owned its own facilities, made its own decisions, and was governed by congregational rule. Any affiliation of that church was with the consent of its members.

I have never been in a Baptist church that took orders from a higher authority within the denomination. I have, however, been a part of affiliated churches that chose to make full use of the services and literature available to us from an association or convention organization. A church can make this choice and still be just as independent as one which makes a different choice.

I think that we have confused the word "independent" with "unaffiliated." Just because a Baptist church chooses not to be affiliated with American, National, Southern, Conservative, Regular, North American, Bible, or any of the many other associations, conventions, or confederations, does not make it any more independent than those who choose to affiliate.

Baptist churches which most loudly proclaim their "independent" status are often, ironically, the churches which may provide the least independence to their members. Often, the self-proclaimed "independent" church becomes very pastor-directed and dogmatic, requiring its members to give up some of their freedom in Christ in order to conform to a narrow, prescribed doctrine. When we label our church as "independent," the term is an obvious redundancy to other Baptists and a warning sign to many others looking for a church with an open door. So the term can work against church growth.

"Bible-believing!" Now there is an adjective that sets Baptists apart. How could there possibly be anything negative about us labeling ourselves as Bible-believing? Who does this term set us apart from? The non-Bible-believers? The Bible-unbelievers? Probably not. As a matter of fact, I have never experienced a church that bragged about being either "non-Bible-believing" or "Bible-unbelieving." Every church of any denomination that I know anything about considers itself Bible-believing and uses the Bible as its basis for belief and doctrine.

To imply, by labeling myself as a Bible-believer, that other Baptists and members of other denominations do not believe the Bible is both erroneous and insulting. When I label myself in this way, I am really saying that only those who agree with my narrow interpretation of Scripture are Bible-believers.

This goes totally against the teaching of Jesus who, in Revelation, described the seven churches which represented the churches then, the churches down through the ages, and the churches now. Jesus said that good and evil, truth and falsehood, and faithful people and unfaithful people were in all of them, with the possible exception of the rich church at Laodicea.

I am afraid that what this term conjures up in the minds of many is that those of us who make a big deal of being Bible-believers may have taken our eyes off God and focused too much on the Bible itself. As a result, instead of seeing the Bible as an instrument that reveals God and points us to him, we may have made it an object of worship. At the very minimum, we are presenting to the world that we are an elitist group who consider ourselves the only ones who really and truly believe the Bible. In either event, we come off as appearing more haughty and militant than humble when we boast that we are a Bible-believing church.

Can you think of a more inappropriate word to use with the gospel of Christ than "conservative"? If we view the term "independent Baptist" as a redundancy, then I hope we will see that the term "conservative Baptist" is an oxymoron. To be conservative means to be inflexible, opposed to change, committed to the present condition, and bound by tradition.

Do you remember what Jesus told the Pharisees when they kept badgering him about not conforming to their conservative, present condition, and inflexible, traditional ways? He told them that new wine could not be put into old wineskins. The power of the new wine would be too great for an inflexible container. Of course, what he was telling them was that the gospel was so powerful that it would literally explode if it was put into the stifling, legalistic, conservative religious system that they had developed.

How can we be proud of an adjective that tells the world that we are just like the Pharisees? We are in favor of maintaining the status quo, preventing change, and maintaining traditions, despite the fact that these characteristics are exactly the opposite of the effects of the gospel.

Paul tells us in 2 Corinthians 5:17: "Therefore, if anyone is in Christ, he is a new creation; the old has gone, the new has come!" The power of the gospel is dynamic. It is dramatic. It is transforming. It will blow the sides off of an old rigid, conservative wineskin.

It can raise the dead, heal the lame, cleanse the leper, feed the hungry, comfort the lonely, and even forgive the sins of people like you and me. It can totally change a life, a marriage, a family, a nation, and the world.

Look at what it did to the Apostle Paul. It changed him from a Pharisee who was trying to stamp out Christianity into its most influential spokesman. Consider Peter. He was changed from a frightened, denying, swearing disciple into a fearless preacher in just a matter of days. He and the other apostles were accused of "turning the world upside down."

Why were Peter, Paul, and the other early Christians persecuted? Not for being conservative! If they were anything, they were revolutionaries for the cause of Christ. There is no indication that they, at any time, were so concerned about not upsetting the status quo or maintaining their traditions that they could be called "old wineskins." The early Christian church was the antithesis of the staid, conservative religious system that Jesus said he could not use as the vessel for his gospel.

What does God want us to be doing in the world today? Certainly not maintaining the status quo. Have you looked around you at the world lately? Things are a mess out there. God wants us to use the gospel to change lives, change hate into love, change war into peace, change selfishness into sacrifice, change suffering into comfort, and on and on. Change—change—change—change—change!

How can we present ourselves to the world as the ones who can help bring about changes offered through the gospel of Christ when we brand ourselves with the term "conservative?" This adjective announces to the same world that we are committed to preventing change?

Some of our adjectives probably serve a useful purpose. The terms "general" and "particular" were used in the "old days" to distinguish between those Baptists who believed that the atonement was for everybody in "general," and those who believed that the atonement was just for the "particular" ones whom God had predestinated.

As I was growing up, I easily understood the differences between the Primitive Baptists, with their strong "sovereignty-of-God" beliefs, and the Freewill Baptists, with their "free-will-of-man" beliefs. In some parts of the country, the term Missionary Baptist distinguishes a congregation from other Baptist congregations who do not believe in missionary endeavors. The adjectives, "American" and "National," work well in this country in identifying two major denominational groups, but may not be an advantage in their efforts to reach the rest of the world. North American Baptists are a group that I learned about only a few years ago.

During the early 1970s when we were living in Florida, I worked with Richard Reed, who had moved to Florida from Texas at the same time we had moved from Ohio. The Reeds were lifelong Southern Baptists, and the Dodds became Southern Baptists when we got to Florida; so Richard and I had a common denominational denominator.

After a number of transfers for us both, I was living in Syracuse, New York, and Richard was living in Bismarck, North Dakota. When we found ourselves together at a meeting in Washington, one of my first questions to him was, "Did you find a Southern Baptist church in Bismarck?"

"Yes," Richard said, "we found one, but we found another Baptist church that we liked better, so we joined it, instead." "What kind of a Baptist church is it?" I asked. "It's a North American Baptist," he replied. "What in the world kind of Baptist is North American Baptist?" I wanted to know. "I've never heard of them." "They are a lot like all the other Baptists, but there is one difference," he said as he started to chuckle. "We send missionaries to Texas." I believe that Richard had gone the complete Baptist circuit: from a Southern Baptist in Texas sending missionaries north, to a North American Baptist in North Dakota sending missionaries south.

It was also while we were living in Florida that I first opened my mouth about the negative aspects of our most detrimental and persistent adjective, "Southern." When our pastor, Brother Jeff Rousseau, reported that there was some sentiment within the Southern Baptist Convention to consider some name other than Southern, it created quite a storm of anger and indignation among our church members. Of course, the people who were indignant were aware of the national and worldwide scope of their denomination and were proud of that. But there was no sentiment, whatsoever, for giving up the term that was sacred to them: Southern.

Being the calm and reasonable person that I am, I tried to relate some of my experiences in the northern parts of the United States and the perception that people "up there" had about Baptists in general and Southern Baptists in particular. I said that to declare yourself to be a Southern Baptist in many parts of the country meant that you were constantly having to explain that you were not associated with some demagogic southern politician; you were assumed to be a racist, so if the person you were trying to witness to was not a racist, you had to try to explain your way out of that trap; and even worse, if the person you were trying to witness to was a racist, you were embraced as a fellow bigot.

Let's face it. We Southern Baptists are associated, rightly or wrongly, with a lot of baggage in the minds of a lot of people including slavery and the Civil War, the Klan, racism, religious intolerance, and regional snobbery. I tried, with no success whatsoever, to make the point that if our goal is to rescue a drowning world with the gospel of Christ, we were not very smart to jump into the water with a millstone around our necks.

I got educated (lambasted?) pretty well about tradition, being the greatest and most blessed group of true believers, and good old southern pride. The consensus was that I did not know what I was talking about and people up north and around the world were fully receptive and anxiously awaiting the opportunity to become Southern Baptists.

My question then was: "How would you react if someone knocked on your door and invited you to a Bible study that was for the purpose of establishing a new Yankee Catholic church in your neighborhood?" I got the immediate knee-jerk reaction that I had hoped for: "I'd tell them that we didn't need them around here." "My point, exactly," I replied.

Why do we persist in identifying ourselves with a term that has negative connotations to millions of the people whom we are trying to reach in this country and that simply sounds like a direction to people in the rest of the world? Would it not help the cause of Christ if the largest of all the groups of us Baptists, the group diligently striving to plant churches throughout the nation, the group with the largest Baptist missionary effort around the world, would identify itself with its vision for the world, rather than its regional past with all of its baggage?

I have not attempted to exhaust the list of adjectives that we Baptists use to identify ourselves that may be offensive or stumbling blocks. I deliberately chose not to discuss one of our worst, "fundamentalist," because I hammered it so hard in the previous chapter. What I have tried to do in this chapter is to force us to think about the way some of the terms that we use cause others to see us.

As you consider my arguments about our adjectives, I urge you to also consider some of the things that Paul said in 1 Corinthians 9:19-23: "Though I am free . . . I make myself a slave to everyone to win as many as possible. To the Jews I became like a Jew to win the Jews. To these under the law I became like one under the law . . . so as to win those under the law. To those not having the law I became like one not having the law . . . so as to win those not having the law. To the weak I became weak, to win the weak. I have become all things to all men so that by all possible means I might save some."

Baptists, if we are going to reach the world for Christ, we will have to realize that the world is not going to beat a path to our door while we are constantly bickering over unimportant theology, showing pride in being traditional and inflexible, clinging to past baggage, and believing that we have God captured in a narrow little box that only we can open.

If, then, the world is not going to come to us, we should be concerned, big time, about how we present ourselves as we go to the world. I believe that the philosophy that Paul expounded in 1 Corinthians is the attitude that God would have us adopt.

If we, as God's people who are called Baptists, would consider our adjectives, and instead of interminably trying to more narrowly define ourselves, we would focus our eyes on the work that we have been called to do, maybe God can still use us to help reach the world for him.

8 ... Would Study the Whole Word of God

HOW BIG IS GOD? HOW MUCH DO WE KNOW ABOUT GOD? DO we have God figured out? Sometimes we hear people say, jokingly, that "God must be a Baptist," or "God is a conservative," or "God is a Republican," indicating that, yes, indeed, they do think that they have God figured out and fitted into their little box. How much do we really understand about God's love, power, and knowledge, or even the subject of this chapter, God's Word?

I knew exactly what a line was until I took geometry in school. Then I found out that what I had thought was a line was, in actuality, a line segment. I learned that a line has no beginning or end. It just keeps going and going until it completes a cycle around the world and, I guess, does it again.

That is the way we are about God and his attributes. We think that we know and understand him when we actually know only a teeny-weeny, infinitesimal, miniscule amount about him. But how much do we comprehend about the unselfish, unmerited love that God offers us? How could we measure our comprehension?

Let us suppose that if we held our hands apart for the distance of a foot, we could be measuring our comprehension of love at, say, age twelve. As we get older and learn more about God, we can spread our hands to, say, eighteen inches. By the time we get married and become parents, our comprehension doubles, at least. That makes it three feet wide. Hopefully, as we continue to grow in our knowledge of God and in our relationships with others, our comprehension extends all the way out to arms length in our lifetime. Is this the extent of God's love?

Of course not! This is merely the limit of our understanding. The love of God has no limits. Like the line, it goes on and on, around the world, around the sun, and on and on around the universe for distances of millions of light years, and we cannot find the beginning of it or the end of it because there is no beginning or end.

We learned a lot about power when we first harnessed a horse, and we still measure power in terms of horsepower. The internal combustion engine made it possible to harness three hundred "horses" and put them under the hood of an automobile. We learned even more about power when we harnessed electricity, and then jet propulsion, and then ultimately, for us to this point, when we unleashed the power of the atom and nuclear energy.

How does this compare to the power of God? We now have the power to blow some big holes in one of the smallest, most inconspicuous, almost unnoticeable specks in the vast universe—Earth. And most of us do not understand even that much power. How, then, can we comprehend the power of God, which, in the past, created an explosion so mighty that it brought the entire universe into being?

And this is not the limit of God's power. Like his love, his power goes on and on, weaving through and around the universe which he created and beyond. His power is limitless.

How much do we know about the knowledge of God? If we amassed the sum total of knowledge of humans since Adam and Eve, we would certainly have a significant line segment, wouldn't we? What if our segment of knowledge reached all the way around the world? Would that be impressive? Yes, until we compared it to the complete and endless knowledge of God which could go around the world tens of thousands of times on its way around the universe and beyond.

How much do we know about the Word of God? Surely he has revealed this to us in its entirety, hasn't he? Doesn't he tell us in the Bible that there cannot be a word added or taken away? Isn't the Bible the whole Word of God?

If you have read this far in this book, you know that Larry Coleman is my favorite preacher hero. I would dedicate this chapter to him if I thought he would endorse it. Since I am not sure about that, I can only give him credit for stimulating my thought process. He did that by preaching a sermon on "the whole Word of God."

His three main points were that God's Word to us consists of God's revelation to us through his written record, the Bible; God's revelation to us through his record in creation; and God's ultimate revelation to us through his Son, Jesus Christ.

Larry's sermon, as you might imagine, featured point number three. This chapter is going to emphasize point number two and go far beyond anything that Larry covered in his sermon. But his sermon helped me to start sorting out things that I had felt were true since I was a child, but had never been able to articulate.

Here goes! Fasten your Baptist safety belts!

My feelings are based on my strong belief, formed at an early age, that the Bible and creation are not in opposition to each other, nor can they be. They are indisputably two different revelations of the same being: Almighty God, the cause-force of the universe. Both revelations have their own strong biblical basis.

We are quick to quote 2 Timothy 3:16 when someone questions the validity of the Bible as the Word of God. Quote it with me: "All Scripture is given by inspiration of God, and is profitable for doctrine, for reproof, for correction, for instruction in righteousness" (KJV).

About the only time we consider Romans 1:20, though, is when we feel compelled to explain to a cynic why the "poor heathens" who have never heard the gospel have to go to hell. "They have nature; that should reveal God to them" is the way Baptists explain how a loving God can send to hell people who have never heard the gospel. It is ironic that some of these same Baptists consider it abominable when scientists try to unlock the mysteries of nature in the world around us.

Let us now look, maybe for the first time in our lives, at Romans 1:20, at a verse directed at us, instead of just pointing it at those who have never been reached by a Baptist missionary: "For the invisible things of him from the creation of the world are clearly seen, being understood by the things that are made, even his eternal power and Godhead; so that they are without excuse" (KJV).

Could this mean that God wants and expects us to understand him through our study of his clearly seen record in creation, and instead of viewing science as the antiChrist, to seek to reconcile these two Words of God—his Word in the Scriptures and his Word in creation?

It has never made any sense to me that God would give us active minds with curiosity about the world around us and then expect us to put our minds into a blind trust when we become Christians. It has been particularly hard for me to watch us turn virtually all Baptist decision making over to the anti-intellectual zealots who have invaded

Baptist life. "Because," we are being told, "the Bible says that things are this way, and you must accept what the Bible says."

The Bible is viewed by many Baptists as the one and only final word on a whole bunch of stuff: the creation, the age of the Earth, the origin of life, why our shin bone is on the front of our leg, etc. I was not very old when I discovered that it was probably not the Bible that was stifling the thought process; it was some of its interpreters. Some interpreters were positive that the world was six thousand years old, and that was that. Some others speculated that if one day is as a thousand years with the Lord, the world could be considerably older than a few thousand years. I decided very early to sit with those behind answer number two.

I have heard some preachers lump all scientists into a category and summarily consign them to hell as atheists. But I have heard some other preachers thank God for the scientists who were finding cures for polio and other dreaded diseases. Even the most virulent anti-scientist preachers could be heard, from time to time, pleading with God to "guide the hands of the surgeons," when someone dear to them was in need of treatment from a medical "scientist."

As Baptists, we pride ourselves on being "a people of the Book," and we are. Some of us even try to go beyond this by calling ourselves "Bible-believing Baptists." We read the Bible from "cover to cover" and study it constantly.

We also occasionally study the Incarnate Word, Jesus Christ, especially around Christmas and Easter. But we have totally neglected any study of the other great Word that God has given us, his record in the creation.

What if God meant what he said in Romans and he really wants us to "see his attributes" by studying his creation? What if we have ignored his wishes and have not learned about him through his creation as he has asked us to do? Are we among the ones who are "without excuse?"

Remember Jesus' answer to the Pharisees when they asked him to quiet the people who were shouting praises to him? He said that if his followers became silent, the stones would cry out. Evidently, when God wants something done, he gets it done, even if the primary provider is unable or unwilling to carry it out.

We need to consider just how unhappy God may be with us for not trying to learn more about him by studying the record that he left us in his creation. Maybe, just maybe, because of our closed minds, he has had to use others.

We call people theologians who devote their lives to the study of God's Word in the Scriptures, and we consider them to be God's servants, or, rather, we consider those who agree with us to be God's servants. We call people scientists who devote their lives to the study of God's Word in the creation, and, as strange as it seems, we often consider them the enemies of God. Wouldn't it be a hoot if the scientists knew more about God than the theologians? And, in some cases, that may be a real possibility.

Australian physicist, Paul Davies, the 1995 winner of the Templeton Prize for Progress in Religion, is of the opinion that science offers a surer path to God than religion. This concept, which should stop us in our tracks, is advanced by a man who follows Billy Graham and Mother Teresa, among others, as a recipient of the Templeton Prize.

Can we say, with any conviction whatsoever, that the theologians who, down through the centuries, have ridiculed, tortured, and killed scientists for studying the creation had a clearer vision of God or a greater knowledge of God than did their victims?

Is there any way that we can defend the actions of religious leaders who have demanded adherence to ignorant contentions that the Earth was flat, the Earth was square, the Earth was the center of the universe, and countless other equally erroneous beliefs simply because they relied solely on their narrow interpretation of the written Word and refused to give any consideration, whatsoever, to the emerging truths of the creation Word?

What are we afraid of? Why do we roll up into a ball and start sucking our thumbs every time anyone mentions a new scientific discovery?

Listen, Baptists. If God made it, then the more we can know about his creation, the more we will know about him; and that should be a good thing, not something to fear. Let us take a look at what we can learn about God from his Word in creation, as interpreted by his servants, the scientists.

I grew up in a hollow in West Virginia. I spent a lot of time playing in the creeks that flowed through our farm. I was always intrigued by the rocks in the creek, which changed dramatically after every "gully washer" as the torrents from the mountains washed away some of the old rocks and brought in a whole new crop.

Some of the rocks were conglomerates composed primarily of little seashells, and yet they washed out of the Appalachian Mountains. How did they get there?

I was particularly fascinated by the rocks which were pieces of slightly off-round cylinders about four inches in diameter with beautiful, patterned lines and indentations that I would find in the little creek above our barn. As kids, we decided that they must be pieces of petrified snakes.

I have one of those stones on my desk at this moment, serving as a bookend. Not until years later did I see similar stones in a museum and learn that they were really pieces of giant fern stems from the Carboniferous Period. How old are they? How did they get there?

One of my favorite places, as a teenager, was my brother's mountaintop farm. From the vantage point of some of his fields, I could look out for miles over deep, dark, wooded valleys and see other plateau areas with old barns and rail fences that identified the homesteads of some of the old-timers of the area. It was always a thrill, after climbing the steep inclines from our creek-bottom farm, to get to the top of the mountain and see the expanses of gently rolling farmland.

There was so much evidence all around me of the antiquity of the Earth that I had trouble reconciling what I saw and what the preachers were telling about the Earth. There were vast deposits of coal and natural gas deep under the ground in West Virginia. How did those deposits get there? The preachers had an immediate answer to that one: "God put them there for man's benefit," I was told. I had no trouble with that. I knew that God put them there, but I wondered why he would just arbitrarily stuff them there six thousand years ago.

That was when I came up with the theory that God created the Earth with the appearance of age. What a discovery! God made the Earth six thousand years ago, I reasoned, complete with coal deposits, pockets of natural gas, pools of oil, lots of fossils, seashells in the mountains, and petrified snakes in the creeks, all of which gave the appearance of having been developed over a long period of time. I could almost hear God chuckling as he watched those stupid scientists, whom I had heard the preachers talking about, trying to figure out his creation.

I was amazed as an adult to find that some Baptist colleges and seminaries actually teach what my juvenile mind thought up by the time I was ten years old, but rejected by the time I was eleven. I rejected my "appearance-of-age" theory for a very logical reason: I figured that God would not lie to us. If he placed false evidence in his creation, that would be dishonest. I believed then and I believe now that God has not lied to us through his Word, the Bible, and I could not conceive then or now of God lying to us through his Word, the creation.

I went away to college and, after being duly warned not to let those liberal science professors shake my faith, went ahead and boldly majored in the agricultural and biological sciences. I especially enjoyed the courses that I took in agronomy and soils. I was fascinated to learn about how the landscapes and formations that made up the environment where I had grown up had come to be.

I learned that five hundred million years ago, the area where I grew up was under the Appalachian Sea. Wow! That was where the seashells in the rocks came from. I learned that the Carboniferous Period was a fifty-or-sixty-million-year period about three hundred million years ago. Double wow! That was how old my "petrified snake" turned out to be.

I found out why the valleys were so deep. It turns out that New River, which is only twenty miles downstream from my boyhood home, was named very inappropriately because, rather than being new, it is the oldest river in the western hemisphere and probably the second oldest river in the world; so the streams around home had been cutting down through the landscape for an awfully long time.

I discovered that this ancient New River which flows north out of North Carolina, north up through Virginia and southern West Virginia, once continued to flow north to a northeastern outlet to the ocean. The northward flow was interrupted many thousands of years ago by the glaciers which covered the northern parts of what is now the United States, creating a great lake which eventually spilled over in a westerly direction and gradually found its way south to the Gulf of Mexico in a path that we now call the Ohio and Mississippi Rivers.

I found that the flat tops of some of the mountains around home were the remnants of a once much smoother, prehistoric landscape and that the reason that these areas had not eroded away into the steep hills and valleys like the rest of the terrain was because they were underlain by a very hard, erosion-resistant sandstone. I found that the soil on these old mountaintop plateaus had its dull gray color because it had been in place for many thousands of years, so long, in fact, that all the iron compounds which normally give soil its color had leached out of it. I was amazed at how many answers I found to my boyhood questions by a basic study of God's Word in creation.

I chose a career as a soil conservationist, and worked for many years in a scientific profession based on knowledge which comes from a study of just one of God's great creations, the soil. The study of soils can tell us a lot.

Soil scientists can determine where the soil came from, how it got there, what it was formed from, its chemical composition, its particle size, and its relationships to other parts of a landscape. Soil interpreters can take that information and predict crop yields, wet or dry basements, stable or high maintenance highways, suitability of the soil for earthen fills and dams, need for irrigation, and hundreds of other interpretations based on particular soil properties.

A few years ago, when we were starting a county-wide soil survey in Clinton County, New York, we began the work with a "first acre ceremony." Since this was a joint county, state, and federal venture, we invited government officials, media representatives, and the interested public so everyone would understand the process and we could map the first acre as they watched.

We selected a site with the beautiful Lake Champlain to our east and the picturesque Adirondack Mountains to our west, and were pleased to have a good crowd show up. I made my little speech, the state commissioner of agriculture spoke, and the chairman of the county soil and water conservation district spoke. Then we turned the program over to Val Krawicki, the soil scientist who would be in charge of the five-year survey.

Val took us to a pit that he had dug and started into a typical scientist's sequential dialogue of the soil-survey process, the tools of the trade, and the various layers of soil that were revealed in the pit profile. About the time he finished describing how a spade was used and started describing, in metric and scientific Latin terms, the characteristics of each soil layer, the television tripods were being folded and most of the media people were heading for their vehicles.

Then a critical question was asked from the audience. "Did I hear you say that there was both a marine layer and a lacustrine layer in that pit?" the person asked. "Are you saying that some of the soil here was deposited in sea water and some in fresh water?"

"Yes," Val replied. Then he launched into a very learned discussion of the effects of the glaciers, when they were here, how thick they were, which mountains they covered, how much their weight had compressed the earth permitting the ocean to come in after the glacier receded, and subsequent fresh water inundation after the ocean had receded, and how the earth is still "rebounding" or slowly rising as it recovers from the weight of the glacier that was once here. He said that the compression of the clay subsoil by the tremendous weight of the glacier was the cause of the familiar "hardpan" at a depth of about thirty six inches that neither roots nor shovels could penetrate.

When Val started this explanation, the tripods were quickly reset, television cameras were clicked on again, and pencils and pads were furiously put to use. We got a full five minutes on the evening news on both the Plattsburg, New York, and Burlington, Vermont, television stations, and none of us officials was even mentioned. The soil scientist and his knowledge of just one tiny portion of the creation—the soil at one spot on the Earth's surface—made the news.

If we dare to look outside the tiny box that some of us think we have God in, and try to see him as he really is, and look at some things which he has revealed through the interpreters of his Word in creation, the scientists, we will find that we have a mighty God, indeed. We will begin to realize that God is not confined to our box, nor is he confined to our Earth. Although our understanding of him is limited, he is unlimited, covering the universe and far, far beyond.

I think that the greatest mystery in the entire universe is why this great God would be concerned about this little speck called Earth and, even more baffling, why he would even notice one of the billions of tiny creatures moving around on the little speck. And to think that he knows how many hairs each of us tiny creatures has on his/her head. And, mystery of mysteries, why he would love us tiny creatures so much that he would take on the form of one of us, live among us, and even die for us.

God's Word in the Scriptures tells us that he is the originator and creator of all things. The Scriptures, however, do not tell us when he did these things, and they are very sketchy as to how he accomplished them. If God wants us to know more about him by learning what he has revealed about when and how he accomplished his creation, then we must, as Paul tells us in Romans, look at the record that he left us in his creation.

God's Word in the creation tells us that he began creating a long, long time ago. Stars have been discovered in the universe that are seventeen billion light years from the Earth. This means that those stars have been shining for seventeen billion years in order for the light to arrive here on Earth. This means that the universe has to be at least seventeen billion years old. That's 17,000,000,000 years old! That's the Word of the Lord, as recorded in creation.

If you want to get an idea of how large the universe must be, you can do a simple math problem of multiplying the speed of light (186,300 miles per second) times the number of seconds in a year (31,536,000) times 17,000,000,000. The answer will be in miles.

And that just measures the distance from the Earth to the most distant stars which have been detected, so far. And that is just looking in one direction. The Earth is not the center of the universe, but neither is it the edge of it, so the size is much larger than the math problem you just solved.

God's record in the creation indicates that the creation began suddenly. Some scientists call this beginning the "big bang." God has left a number of ways in which this sudden act of creation can be determined. The rate of expansion of the universe can be measured and then reversed through the use of computers to study how a decreasing universe can be seen as coming together like a movie being run backwards. The unfathomable power of the original explosion of the mighty forces of heat and light that occurred at the creation is still detectable as sound waves in the universe.

God has provided us with many ways to calculate the age of the Earth. Geologists have developed an understanding of the rates of sedimentation, and can calculate time by studying the layers of soil and rock on the Earth's surface. I love geologists. The rocks really do cry out to the glory of God, and the geologists are the ones who hear them and interpret their messages to us.

Other scientists have studied the saltiness of the world's oceans and calculated time by determining how long it has taken for fresh water accumulating in the great oceans to reach the present level of saltiness through evaporation.

The most accurate record found so far that God has left us in his creation to determine the age of the Earth is in the rocks. By determining the amount of lead produced by the decay of uranium in a rock and comparing it to the other forms of lead in the rock, the age of the rock can be accurately calculated. Using this method, rocks have been found on Earth that are more than 3.5 billion years old.

So, is this the age of the Earth? Probably not, because the astronauts have brought back rocks from the moon, and they are about 4.5 billion years old. So, if God created the Earth and the moon at the same time, the moon rocks, from a much more stable and unchanging environment would be a better guide. The age of the moon rocks turned out to be the same age as meteors which have hit the Earth, further evidence of the time of the Earth's creation. So, the record in the creation that God left us indicates that he created the Earth about 4.5 billion years ago.

As every school child who has looked at a globe of the world knows, if you were to remove the Atlantic Ocean, North and South America would fit very nicely up against Europe and Africa. God's Word in the creation explains that they appear this way for a very good reason; they used to be connected.

As a matter of fact, God's Word in the creation tells us that all the land areas of the world today were, at one time, all a part of one large land mass. This mass began breaking up about two hundred million years ago in sort of a twisting motion, breaking North America from Europe, South America from Africa, Antarctica and Australia from South America, and eventually, Australia from Antarctica, with India breaking off from Africa and crashing into southern Asia.

This movement is like the expansion of the universe in that it is still going on. This is evidenced by numerous earthquakes at critical points where the various plates of the Earth collide, scrape, and otherwise interact, resulting in upheavals at the Earth's surface. Another way of describing the movement of the Earth's continents is that the distance from Europe to America is a few inches farther now than when Columbus came in 1492. Another example is that the activity along the San Andreas fault will, if the Lord tarries, result in Los Angeles moving up the west coast past San Francisco on its way to Alaska in a few million years.

We know from the Bible that God created every living thing. What does his record in creation tell us about his creation of life? Most of the clues that God has given us in his creation indicate that he first created life in the sea, so this is as good a place to study God's Word in creation as anywhere on Earth.

One of the most dramatic and accurate places on Earth to study God's Word in creation is the Grand Canyon of the Colorado River. The Grand Canyon is nearly one mile deep and cuts through two billion years of the Earth's natural history. The layers of sedimentary rocks that were laid down over billions of years when the area was under the sea have been remarkably stable through the millennia and serve as a fascinating record of life on Earth.

A study of the Grand Canyon tells us that God created the most simple forms of life first. The layers at the bottom of the canyon contain only fossils of tiny microscopic beings. This tells us that there was life two billion years ago, but it was very primitive.

How did God create the first microscopic being? What material did he use? What process did he use to cause that first moment of life? I do not know the answers to these questions, but there are scientists who are seeking the answers.

Let us assume for a moment that scientists discover information that tells them that he used sea water, complex proteins, amino acids, and a lightning bolt to first create life in a single cell. Would that diminish God?

Who made the sea water, the complex proteins, the amino acids, and the lightning bolts? Would the Creator of those things, then, not be free to use them, if he so chose, to create life? What if this is one of his "invisible attributes" that he wants us to see?

Was the creation of the first single-celled life form any less a miracle than the creation of Adam? God used the same material, the elements occurring in the Earth's surface, to create both. Is it possible that, in the mind of God, once Earth materials were combined with his life-giving power, Adam and all other life forms were already created? Would you "unaccept" Jesus as your Lord and Savior if God's Word in creation eventually showed this to be the case?

As we come up through the layers and the millennia of records of the Grand Canyon, God, the Creator, reveals to us that he kept very busy. By the time we get to the layers deposited four hundred to five hundred million years ago, he reveals that he has created quite a variety of aquatic plant and animal life, including shellfish, and even some fish with backbones. As we come on up to the top of the canyon and its records of about two hundred million years ago, there are fossils of an even wider variety of sea plants and animals, land plants like ferns, amphibians which could live out of the water, and numerous insects.

What, then, has God revealed about himself to us through his Word recorded in the Grand Canyon? His creation of life began more than two billion years ago. He began his creation with the very simplest form of life, and probably created it in the sea. His creation process was continuous, becoming ever more diverse and complex. He was still creating new critters until as recently as two hundred million years ago, at least.

It seems to me that the three greatest stumbling blocks that we face in reconciling God's Word in the Scripture and God's Word in the creation are our beliefs about Charles Darwin, Adam and Eve, and the flood. Poor Charles Darwin. If there has ever been anyone more vilified by Baptist preachers than he has, then it must be the devil himself. I have heard his name thousands of times from Baptist pulpits, and never have I heard one good thing said about him.

Who was Charles Darwin and what did he do? Darwin was an Englishman, a religious man, and a divinity student at Cambridge University, who eventually made the study of nature his life's work. He studied God's creation, recorded it meticulously, and after years of soul searching, finally revealed what he had found.

He recorded his conclusions in a book, *The Origin of Species*, which presents his findings that life on Earth, rather than being static and unchanging, is constantly undergoing gradual or "evolutionary" changes in response to environmental conditions and that the plants and animals in any location on Earth evolve to adapt to their environment through a process of natural selection and the survival of the fittest.

He did not arrive at these conclusions easily. He traveled to various places, including South America and, most notably, the Galapagos Islands, to study the uniqueness of plants and animals in various locations. He kept voluminous notes about everything that he observed.

Darwin wrestled with his notes and the best scientific information of his time for a period of five years before he could fully accept what he had learned about the creation. Even then, he said that revealing what he had discovered was like confessing to a murder.

As painful as it was for Darwin, he did the world a great favor. Because of his work and that of others, we can begin to make some sense out of some of the great mysteries of the world, like the vast differences between the plants and animals of Australia and New Zealand and those in the rest of the world.

Those areas broke off from Antarctica and South America at a time when the life forms that God had created were relatively primitive. As the life forms became increasingly more complex, they were drastically different from the more complex life forms on the other continents. The patterns in the primitive life forms were copied in the more complex life forms which were created later. For example, virtually every mammal in Australia is a marsupial, an oddity in most of the rest of the world.

A visit to any other isolated spot on Earth further confirms the observations of Darwin. What does all this mean?

It means that old Charley observed things as they were and accurately recorded them, and we have to deal with that. Or, rather, we should deal with that. Charles Darwin, a theologian turned scientist, learned more about how God works in the world around us in his lifetime of studying God's Word in the creation than theologians had learned in a thousand years of studying God's Word in the Scriptures.

Regardless of whether we consider Darwin to be the devil incarnate or God's servant, many aspects of our lives are dependent on our use of the results of his work and resultant scientific endeavors based on his findings. One of the most important people who built on Darwin's work and began the scientific field of genetics was another religious man, a monk named Gregor Mendel.

By injecting the creativity of man into the process described by Darwin to speed up or otherwise manipulate the changes that occur between generations, we now have Santa Gertrudis cattle, Landrace hogs, hybrid corn, dairy herds producing twenty thousand pounds of milk per cow, seedless oranges, frost-free strawberries, designer tomatoes, turkeys with breasts so large they cannot stand up if permitted to grow to adulthood, beefaloes, big dogs, little dogs, hunting dogs, racing dogs, lap dogs, show dogs, killer dogs, skinny chickens which lay lots of eggs, heavy chickens which produce lots of meat, long-legged sheep, short-legged sheep, small, fast race horses, large, strong draft horses, high-yielding varieties of grains, and on and on through a seemingly endless list of new breeds of animals and varieties of plants.

Many of these changes have come within our lifetimes, so we have seen them, and even worked to make them happen; they cannot be denied. If this much change has happened over such a short time span, how can we deny that massive changes have occurred in life on Earth over the past two billion years or so?

There is also a down side to these changes that we have observed in our lifetimes. I no longer grow potatoes in my garden because the

Colorado Potato Beetle is so prolific in this area and the beetles have evolved and become immune to the pesticides which used to kill them. Many flies, mosquitos, and other insects have changed or evolved enough that the substances which once killed them are ineffective.

And if we think that insects change fast, what about germs and viruses? Some of our greatest health dangers are disease-causing agents which can no longer be controlled by antibiotics.

Shortly after our son Mike married Kaye, he was suffering with what he thought to be a bad cold when he suddenly became critically ill. We got him to an emergency room in minutes and then worried and prayed as an army of doctors worked with him.

Miraculously, he survived and made a full recovery from a form of pneumonia caused by a streptococcus that was resistant to antibiotics. We were reminded of the peril that Mike was in when, one month later, the world was shocked by the death of Muppet creator Jim Henson from the same type of pneumonia.

How do bacteria and viruses get that way? They change! They evolve! The few individual organisms which are not affected by the antibiotic survive the treatment and multiply. Since the vulnerable organisms are killed, the new "virulent" strain replaces them and thrives.

That is natural selection and the survival of the fittest. I can almost hear old Charley chuckling.

What about Adam and Eve? What has years of study of God's Word in the creation revealed about them? God's Word in creation convinced a group of scientists in 1991 that all people on Earth are the descendents of a single woman who lived in Africa whom those scientists called "Eve."

A lot of methods were used to arrive at these conclusions based on the record in the creation: archeological studies, fossil records, anthropological studies, statistical analyses, placenta studies of new mothers from different races and cultures around the world, and genetic mutation frequency studies, to name a few.

Well, I have finally found something that scientists and "God-in-a-box" Baptists can agree on. Or have I? The big disagreement about Eve between scientists and God-in-a-boxers would be when she lived. Some of God's servants interpreting the Bible would say that she was here six thousand years ago, while others interpreting the creation would say that she was here about two hundred thousand years ago.

And what about Adam? Those scientists could not account for him. The evidence that they have found pointed to a single female entity as the start of the human race.

Recently, other scientists using similar methods have concluded that our first human ancestor was a man who lived about 270,000 years ago. Was this Adam? Where was Eve? Why do two similar studies lead to two different genders? Did Adam live alone for seventy thousand years?

The Bible tells us that God created Eve from Adam in some sort of a divine cloning operation. Since clones have the exact genetic makeup as the original organism, maybe they are indistinguishable in the creation record.

That brings me to the flood, and I may have saved the most difficult for last. People are so desperate to "prove" the flood that we hear constantly of expeditions, fly-over attempts, and studies of aerial photography, all in hopes of finding some piece of the ark.

I remember, many years ago, that there was some discussion among Baptists as to what constituted the "world" which was destroyed by the flood. Was it the entire globe or the known world of the time? But after the onslaught of the "red hots" from fundamentalist Baptist colleges, and the subsequent emulation of those institutions by previously more open Baptist schools, such discussion seemed to disappear.

Some serious discrepancies exist between the way most Baptist preachers whom I have known interpret God's biblical record of the flood and the record that God provides us in his creation. The typical Baptist preacher version of the flood goes something like this: The water covered the entire globe four thousand years ago. I have even heard sermons that the entire globe was destroyed and that God had to create a whole new one before the ark could land. All animal life on the entire globe was destroyed, except for the animals which Noah took with him into the ark. All people on Earth except Noah and his family were killed. And all living people and animals on Earth are the descendents of the occupants of the ark.

God's record in his creation tells the story differently. Sorry, Baptists, God did not leave any indication in his Word in creation that the entire globe was covered with water four thousand years ago.

God did leave a clear record in his natural Word, however, that there was a great flood forty-eight hundred years ago which covered the entire Sumerian civilization region served by the Tigris and Euphrates Rivers. This is the area, the Bible tells us, where Noah's great grandson, Nimrod, began a settlement which would become the kingdom of Babylon, the first of the great civilizations of the western world.

There is no record in God's Word in creation that the lives of all of the world's animals were snuffed out. His natural Word, instead, shows that the kangaroos lived in Australia for thousands of years before the flood and continued to live there after the flood. The descendents of the bison that were roaming the great plains of the western hemisphere for thousands of years before the flood continue to roam to this day. To put it another way, God tells us through his creation that the great diversity of hundreds of thousands of different species of animals and plants was not globally destroyed.

God's Word in the creation does indicate that all people on Earth have descended from one woman, but that woman could not be Noah's wife, who lived a mere four or five thousand years ago. There is evidence in the creation that my American Indian ancestors were roaming around Summers County, West Virginia, twelve to fifteen thousand years ago, and their descendents were still there when my Scotch-Irish forebears started to settle the region in the eighteenth century.

Consider the many thousands of years that the Aborigines of Australia and other native peoples of the world have lived continuously in their environment. What, then, are my conclusions about the flood? Did it occur? Did God lie to us in the Bible? Yes, it occurred. God says so in his Word in Scripture and in his Word in creation.

I believe, as the Bible says, that Noah, his family, and a large group of animals were preserved on the ark. And I hope that someone eventually confirms this through God's Word in creation by finding remnants of the ark.

I believe that God used the flood to demonstrate his judgment, his punishment of sin, his saving grace, and his provision for his own. The lessons which God has taught us are the same whether the flood covered a country, a continent, the globe, or the universe. He could have done any of the above. Remember, he is God. His Word in the creation tells us which he chose.

No. God did not lie in the Bible, but neither did he lie in his creation. Both revelations are telling the truth. If I believe that God is both the inspirational Author of Scripture and also the Creator, I must accept that both are true.

Where does this leave us, then. I think that we need to begin to rethink the points of discussion and reconciliation that we were discussing before we were so rudely interrupted by the anti-intellectual movement which has taken over the majority of Baptist life. The record of the Scripture and the creation were written by the same author. They cannot be in conflict.

Our Bible schools and seminaries need to provide, as a minimum, some education about God's Word in the creation. The ignorance and naivete of some of our preachers is embarrassing. They know so little about science that they are gullible to "holyspeak" hucksters promoting everything from quack herbal remedies to snappy answers about age-old questions concerning the creation.

I recall one pastor who was looking so weak and sick one Sunday morning that I did not think he would be able to conduct the service. When I asked him what was wrong, he replied, "I'm just having a little trouble adjusting to my new 'diet regimen.' I am taking a 'cleanser' that is purging all the poison from my system, and, man, is it rough."

"What on earth kind of garbage are you taking?" I asked, "Did a doctor prescribe it?" "No, Brother Paul," he responded, "but there is nothing to worry about, for it is all herbal and has nothing in it but natural ingredients." "That's what they told Socrates," I yelled. "Why else do you think he was stupid enough to drink the hemlock?"

Baptists, the conflict is not between the Bible and creation. The conflict is within us and our narrow-mindedness and shortsightedness. Baptists, we do not have to be dumb to be Christians.

If God's people who are called Baptists would study the whole Word of God, seeking to know him from his Word both in Scripture and in creation, and measure all of our actions by the example of the ultimate Word of God, the Incarnate Christ, then we could rejoice when God permits scientific advances, instead of clinging to narrow positions that diminish the image of God which we present to the world.

9   ... WOULD LIVE IN HARMONY

I WAS RAISED IN A HARD-WORKING, RELIGIOUS FAMILY. WHEN asked to describe my parents, I have often said that my mother was very religious and my father was a Baptist.

What I mean by that statement is that my mother's religion, born of her strict Methodist upbringing, was on the inside and the outside. She lived it, she talked it, she walked it.

Dad, on the other hand, was more of a "pray-in-the-closet" Baptist who lived an exemplary Christian life and was a leader in church and denominational affairs, but he was much less vocal than Mom about telling you how good God was being to him at the moment.

I was reminded of my parents a few years ago at the wedding of my preacher hero, Larry Coleman, and his beautiful bride Kim, who was a devout member of the Church of the Nazarene. One comment overheard at the wedding reception was, "I sure hope they get along. Kim is so much more religious than Larry, you know."

My dear, devout mother sure knew how to put a spiritual expectation on a kid. Since I was a "change-of-life" baby who had brothers in high school when I was born, Mom felt that I was special, born for a special purpose, and told me that nearly every day of my life. Named after the Apostle Paul, no less, I was destined to do great things for the Lord, according to my mother.

I cannot even imagine the relationship between the boy Jesus and Mary, his mother. Boy, did she have some stuff to tell him—announced by an angel, miraculously conceived, named by the angel, and destined to ascend to the throne of David and rule over the house of Jacob forever. Mary must have told Jesus about the shepherds and the Wise Men coming to Bethlehem, Simeon and Anna recognizing him as the Promised One at the Temple when he was an infant, their escape to Egypt to save his life, and many other stories. Is it any wonder that he was a precocious child at age twelve, his divine nature notwithstanding?

Dad's expectations for me were that I would always "work harder" and "do better." No task that I ever carried out was done quite well enough or fast enough. No report card was ever greeted with any higher praise than "that's pretty good, but I see room for improvement." Being born during the Great Depression in one of the poorest sections of the country only served to accentuate the importance of Dad's uncompromising standards of hard work and achievement.

Thus, I grew into adulthood with two powerful sets of expectations. Mom had me convinced that I was placed on the earth for the purpose of doing "God's work." Dad had me convinced that I needed to combine education, hard work, and a steady profession in order to "amount to something."

I have spent the greatest part of my adult life trying to live up to those two sets of expectations. The strategy that I developed was to work as hard as I could all week in school or on the job, and then do as much of "God's work" as possible on Sunday.

As a result, I gained a wonderful education and had a successful career in federal government service. Dad's two proudest days, as far as I was concerned, were when I entered graduate study at Harvard University and when I became the state conservationist for New York.

But I never let any grass grow under my feet on Sundays, either. I have never been away from church. I accepted Christ in, and became a member of, an American Baptist church. Since then, as I have moved around the country, I have been a member of a Bible Baptist Fellowship church, a Conservative Baptist of America church, and four Southern Baptist churches.

I have taught, preached, prayed, led the music, directed choirs, played the piano, visited, witnessed, conducted nursing-home services, directed youth programs, held retreats, served as a deacon and a trustee, cleaned the church, mowed the lawn, worked in the nursery, and coached the softball team.

You name it, I've done it. (Hey! I should remember all of this, just in case I am the unfortunate one who has to follow the Apostle Paul at the judgment. I wonder which of the apostle's acts of sacrifice equate to coaching a softball team?)

However, I can see now that I was not in true harmony with myself, because I had accepted what I perceived to be two separate sets of expectations from my parents, and was trying to accomplish both. What I was missing was that they did not have to be, nor should they be, separate. They could, and should, be harmoniously combined into a single purpose for my life.

Three things occurred which have helped me to understand this. I hope they will be of help to you if you have felt, as I did, that unless you are a preacher or a missionary, you have to do secular work part of the time and "God's work" part of the time.

My first revelation was when I heard a definition of harmony that I liked. I do not remember the source, nor the exact wording, but I got the meaning. Harmony exists when each and every part of God's creation is carrying out the function for which it was created.

I thought and thought about that definition. Does this mean that every plant and every creature is created for a purpose, even poison ivy and chiggers? Does this mean that every person on the face of the Earth has a purpose and function? Does this mean that God has a plan for every individual's life—every person, and not just me? If God intended for everybody to do his work, wouldn't the pulpits be crowded?

I loved the definition and the concept, but I was not able to fully comprehend it. Then I received revelation number two at, of all places, a swearing-in ceremony of the New York State Bar Association.

While I was in high school, and again while I was an undergraduate in college, I had seriously considered studying law. Of all the options open to me, this was the one which most distressed my mother. With her "holy-life" model for the Christian, she simply could not see how lawyers could ever get into heaven, considering the way she thought that they had to be a bit loose with the truth.

When both of our sons expressed their intentions to go to law school, I dutifully shared with each their late grandmother's misgivings about their chosen profession. I also told them that since she had never practiced law and was, therefore, undoubtedly in heaven, she just might be watching them.

With this as my background, I went to the ceremony where Doug was to be admitted to the New York State Bar Association, without even an inkling that I was about to receive a revelation. The main speaker was some important, prestigious judge from Rochester. I thought for a minute that I was in the wrong place. I thought that I was hearing an address to the graduating class of a seminary or a newly ordained bunch of preachers.

"Yours is the most important profession on Earth," the judge told them. "There is a greater need for your services now than at any time in our history." He proceeded to describe examples of injustice in our society and explain how the practice of law and the judicial system could right these wrongs. He urged them to be honest, diligent, and ethical. He challenged them to change the world and make it better.

I simply had never thought about lawyers and the practice of law being the great hope of improving our society. But the judge was so good that he convinced me, almost.

What has fully convinced me, however, is watching Doug serve as an honorable member of an honorable profession. And now Mike is also helping to improve the lives of people by providing them with competent, ethical legal representation.

The judge was right. For those people who are created to practice it, the law is the greatest profession in the world, and it can make the world a better place. I do not think that the boys have forgotten either their grandmother or getting into heaven.

Doug, especially, detests lawyer jokes. Yet, one day he said, "Dad, I heard a lawyer joke that I think Grandma would have liked." It seems that this lawyer dies and arrives at the Pearly Gates, where he is greeted by St. Peter. St. Peter checks his list and tells the lawyer that he is on the list and can go on into heaven. "Are you sure?" the lawyer asks. "I am very surprised by all this."

"Now, now," St. Peter said, patronizingly, "don't be too surprised. Contrary to what some people think, we do have a few lawyers who make it." "That's not it," said the lawyer. "It's just that I am so young. I am only thirty years old." "Why, how can that be?" asked St. Peter. "We totaled up your billing hours and decided that you had to be at least eighty."

My third revelation occurred at the New York Agricultural Research Center at Geneva. Mario Cuomo, then governor of New York, was giving a speech, congratulating the researchers and scientists for their award-winning work. "You are doing marvelous work here at Geneva," the governor said, "You are developing more productive crops, crops which are more resistant to disease and insects, and crops which are more nutritious." In fact, "Through your genetic research and other breakthrough technologies, you are opening up whole new worlds of potential ways of producing food and other agricultural products," he continued.

Then the revelation came. "The work that you are doing here at Geneva will help feed starving children, provide better nutrition for nursing mothers, and reduce the risk of crop failure for struggling farmers in places all around our world," he said. "No other task on Earth is more important than the work that you are doing here. You are truly doing God's work."

What a discovery! Here were people doing God's work and none of them was a preacher. They were not in church, and it was Thursday, not Sunday. And I did not even know if any of them were Baptists.

I knew that I had to rethink what is really meant by "God's work." I had been operating on the assumption that God's work was preaching, praying, witnessing, attending, teaching, singing, tithing, etc. Now I was beginning to realize that I had been missing the boat all my life. God's work is not just what we do in church.

As a matter of fact, that may not be God's work for some of us at all. Some of us are ill-suited for church activities other than quiet worship, but that does not mean that God does not have a great plan for our lives and great things which he expects us to do.

My brother-in-law Ralph is awfully quiet about his faith. He accompanies my sister Rhodetta to church and even sits on the front row to be near her while she directs the choir, plays the organ, and otherwise helps to run things in their church.

I warned Ralph that he ran the risk, by sitting up front in church, of being asked by the preacher to "lead in prayer." He replied, "If he asks me, I'll do what Nancy Reagan said to do. I'll just say no!"

But this good man is up at the crack of dawn every day to do things for others. He goes to the home of his aged father and step-mother and fixes breakfast. He checks on others in his community who are in need at the moment.

He became the "adopted son" for the local bar owner who had become old and disabled. Ralph spent many days and drove many miles to see that he got adequate medical treatment and that his last days on earth were as comfortable as possible. He has also become the "adopted son" of a retired preacher in his community, taking him and his wife on trips and including them in family activities.

At the request of an aunt who was terminally ill, he managed her affairs and arranged for her terminal care and funeral. He did these things completely out of love because he knew that she had chosen, for some reason, not to include him in her will.

Ralph gets called in the middle of the night to come and help an older person get another disabled person back into bed after the person has fallen. He arranges for people who need treatment to get the treatment and takes them there. He helps arrange for social services assistance in the home for persons needing it.

But, "lead in prayer in a church service?"—probably not in our lifetime. But think about it. Who is doing more of God's work, the person who prays a long public prayer or the person who works to meet the needs of persons around him/her? Rhodetta and I have talked often that Ralph's eulogy should just be the story of the Good Samaritan.

Remember, the church is not our mission field. We are not called to "go ye into all the churches." The world is our mission field. The world is where we are to do the bulk of God's work, not in the church. Yes, the church should be our empowerment, our home base, our recharge station, but the world must be our mission. God so loved the world.

Let me summarize what I learned through the three revelations. When we are doing work which benefits others, we are doing God's work. What would he be doing if he were here, bodily? He would be feeding, healing, comforting, sharing, helping, supporting, and otherwise unselfishly serving other people. That is what he did when he was here, and that is what he has created us to do, on his behalf.

When we are carrying out the functions which God has created us to do, we are in harmony with the rest of his creation. God has a unique and distinctive plan for each person, and he calls us and will equip us and lead us if we will yield to his will.

Any profession which can be used for the benefit of others, rather than solely for personal gain or at the expense of others, is God's work, if practiced honorably. This means that doing the work that you love may be your main purpose in life. That may be the reason that God has created you and placed you on the earth.

This means that I can look back at my life's work and reflect that when I worked with others to conserve the soil which produces the food that people eat, when we worked to protect the quality of water that people drink, when we worked to reduce the flooding of people's homes and businesses, and when we worked to improve the economic conditions of people needing help, I was doing God's work.

This was the work that God had created me for, had prepared me for, led me into, and helped me to accomplish. He had not created me for the pulpit, or the monastery, or the seminary; but the role for which he created me was, in no way, any less his work.

Rose and I have become aware of people whom we observe doing God's work, especially since our sensitization due to her accident and illness. We knew immediately that the emergency crew and the surgeon who saved her life after her accident were doing God's work.

But then, as we looked around us, we saw countless others also doing God's work: the nurses aide who changed the beds, the sensitive nurse who realized the need for comfort in the middle of the night, our family members who rallied around us, the friends who helped, the person who heard about Rose from the friend of a friend and wrote such a helpful letter, my co-worker from two thousand miles away whom I had never met who had special prayer for Rose at her church every Sunday for weeks, the little girl who bought and framed "Footprints in the Sand" and sent it to Rose, our pastor, a woman chaplain, a Catholic priest, the local stake president of the Mormon Church, and countless others whom I will recall later and wish I had included.

Now that our eyes are open, we see people doing God's work every day. We see them building houses, bagging groceries, planting crops, giving blood, pitching a ball to a child, collecting money to help control cancer, picking up litter, recycling waste, repairing cars, cleaning homes, selling appliances, delivering meals on wheels, hauling garbage, befriending both the terminally ill and the mentally ill, visiting the elderly, delivering mail, providing care for the little ones whose parents have other pressing responsibilities, fighting for justice, struggling for equality, teaching school, arresting lawbreakers, ministering to prisoners, helping children cross the street, filling teeth, cleaning clothes, giving shots, counseling the depressed, coaching Little League teams, and loving and supporting their families.

Does this mean that every person in the world is doing God's work? No! But it does mean that every one of us is created to do God's work; we have the potential, and if we will let him lead us, we can be doing his work in harmony with the rest of his creation.

Who are those not doing his work? Who are the people who are out of harmony? The people who are out of harmony are those who are concerned, primarily, with their personal ambitions and personal gain.

The same temptations which the devil tried out on Jesus in the wilderness—power, fame, and personal comfort—are the ones which the devil still uses on us today. All of us, at one time or another, succumb to these temptations. Some, unfortunately, live there all the time.

The public official who is overly concerned about his or her career and status will often let personal ambition overshadow the task of carrying out policies for the public good. The attorney or physician who is motivated by the opportunity to get rich may lose sight of justice and compassion. The farmer who is only concerned about profit may grow crops which harm, rather than benefit, others. The pastor who seeks status and power may sacrifice the opportunity to be a Christ-like servant. The televangelist who becomes greedy may exploit the very people whom God created that evangelist to help. The religious leader who is tempted by the lure of power may alienate many whom God would have him or her serve—by entering into political alliances.

These are just a few illustrative examples of how we can get out of harmony with God's plan for our lives, and out of harmony with the rest of his creation. How do we get into harmony, or back into harmony? Baptists, we really do know the answer to this one.

We must humble ourselves, pray, seek God's face, and turn from our wicked ways. We must accept Christ, not just as our Savior, but also as the Lord and guiding force of our lives. We must be willing to "die daily," so that God the Holy Spirit can live through us. We must live within his will for our lives and do the work for which he has called us.

What happens if we do all this? In times past, I have been troubled by Jesus' statement that we would do greater things than he did while he was on earth. Did he really mean that, or was he just giving a coach's exaggerated pregame pep talk? I believe he meant it, and that the way it can be accomplished is for each of us to live the life for which we were created, working in harmony with the rest of creation.

Jesus fed the four thousand. He fed the five thousand. And those numbers only counted the "worthy" members of the society, the men. Realistically, he fed crowds of ten thousand or more at least two times, and he was working with meager resources.

How can we top that? Think of what would happen if we turned over our vast resources to Christ and let him bless and multiply them.

Remember, we have the capacity, the resources, and the technology to adequately feed every person on earth. Great things are being done by scientists carrying out God's work in the development of crops, nutrition, animal breeding, and natural-resource management. Millions, even billions, are being fed. That is the good news.

The bad news is that there are millions of hungry people in our world at this moment; before this day ends, thousands of people, mostly children, will die of starvation or malnutrition. How are we out of harmony on this most basic of issues, feeding the hungry?

Governments are out of harmony when the only parts of the world that are helped by wealthy countries are those which can provide a military or an economic advantage. Religious denominations and missionary societies are out of harmony when they go only to preach, and ignore the suffering, or choose not to minister in the tough areas altogether. Some televangelists have even been exposed for making a mockery of the situation by showing pictures of the starving children, soliciting millions of dollars, and then using the vast majority of the money contributed for their own opulence. Sometimes they have stooped so low that they have bribed local officials in a needy area to stage photo opportunities which appear to show the evangelists helping the children.

Baptists, if we live in harmony with God's wish that the hungry be fed, we can have an impact on our government's policies, and our denominations and missionary societies can set an example for meeting the physical and spiritual needs of lost and suffering people throughout the world in a balanced way.

Jesus healed the sick. We have, through our medical and scientific efforts, conquered some of the most dreaded diseases that have caused suffering. We no longer fear smallpox or polio. Many childhood diseases which I had to endure are not threats to my grandchildren. People carrying out God's work in medical science are working on cancer, AIDS, heart disease, diabetes, MS, MD, and literally hundreds of other diseases which may also be conquered. New breakthroughs in genetic research may soon usher in a whole new era in the treatment of disease, eclipsing anything that we have ever seen.

Baptists, if we live in harmony with God's wish that the sick be healed, we will support public research, we will contribute to reputable organizations conducting research, and we will work for ways in which everybody can receive the benefits of the healing which God is providing through his servants, the medical scientists. Somehow, I do not believe that God has revealed the secrets of his creation to scientists so only the rich can be healed. That is just not his way.

Jesus struggled against injustice and prejudice. We are privileged to be living in a country with a well-defined system of laws which not only governs our society, but also protects every individual. At its harmonious best, our system of courts and laws can guarantee the rights, the equality, and the full citizenship of all members of our society.

Baptists, we have a heritage of supporting the freedom and rights of individuals. Some of our number were used of God to be the influential advocates of the separation of church and state. Others were used to be the vanguard in the struggle for civil rights for all Americans. We must live in harmony as exemplary citizens of a free country and diligently continue to protect the rights of all individuals.

God granted me the great privilege of having a career doing the work that I was created to do—working with the soil and with other people who also work with the soil by studying it, categorizing it, mapping it, interpreting it, plowing it, tilling it, and harvesting its bounty. God then graciously revealed to me that my work was his work, also.

What about your life's work? Is it his work, too? Do you enjoy your work? Are you good at what you do? Is your work of benefit to others? Are you sure that your work causes no harm to others? Can you do your work "as unto the Lord?"

If you can answer yes to all those questions, you should pause and thank God for his leadership in your life. It sounds like you have found his plan for your life and are being faithful to your calling.

I want to conclude with three passages from the Bible, one from the Old Testament and two from the New Testament, which help summarize not only this chapter, but the entire book as well: (1) Micah 6:8: "He hath showed you, O man, what is good. And what does the Lord require of you? To act justly and to love mercy and to walk humbly with your God"; (2) James 1:27: "Religion that God our Father accepts as pure and faultless is this: to look after orphans and widows in their distress and to keep oneself from being polluted by the world"; and (3) 1 John 4:19-20: "We love because he first loved us. If anyone says, 'I love God,' yet hates his brother, he is a liar. For anyone who does not love his brother, whom he has seen, cannot love God, whom he has not seen."

Baptists, all we have to do to live in harmony is to be just and kind, walk humbly in the will of God, help those in need, and love others the way God loves us and them. I firmly believe that God still has a work for us Baptists to do in the world. But I also firmly believe that if we are going to get this work done, this is where we have to start.